Teach Yourself NUMEROLOGY

LORD GANESHA AT TRINIDAD (WEST INDIES)

Published by :
Lotus Press Publishers & Distributors

Teach Yourself
NUMEROLOGY

Pt. Rajnikant Udadhyaya
Pt. Gopal Sharma

4735/22, Prakash Deep Building
Ansari Road, Darya Ganj,
New Delhi - 110002

Lotus Press : Publishers & Distributors
Unit No. 220, 2nd Floor, 4735/22, Prakash Deep Building,
Ansari Road, Darya Ganj, New Delhi- 110002
Ph.: 41325510, 98118-38000
• E-mail : lotuspress1984@gmail.com
www.lotuspress.co.in

Teach Yourself Numerology

ISBN: 81-8382-038-7

Printed & Published by : **Lotus Press Publisher & Distributors,** New Delhi-02

PREFACE

Numerology, the simplest of the occult sciences to master, offers deep insights into the personality. You can use numerology to understand yourself, friends, associates and lovers. You can see the dynamics of relationships and you can determine the best time to marry, change jobs, move, invest and travel. Numerology is simply the oldest of the divination arts and often the least understood.

This book provides a simple, intelligent, and useful guide which outlines the history, the various systems, as well as the uses and applications of numerology. From numerology as applied to names and what it can tell you, the concept and reality of "lucky" and "unlucky" numbers, and the practical applications of numerology. This book provides readers with a solid understanding, allowing them to utilize and incorporate into their life. Here you will find quick and easy guidance for the meaning of your name, married name, family name and a wealth of information about your birth date. In addition you will find expert instruction on the predictive elements of numerology.

This book is designed by the learned authors to open the readers to a new awareness about the power of numbers and how they influence our lives. It's easy to follow and user friendly.

Dr. B.B. Puri
Chairman, The Research Institute of Vedic Culture

Acknowledgements

Besides all the ancient and modern scholars our deep gratitude and sincere thanks are due to **Dr. D. Poornachandra Rao,** The noted Feng-Shui Master & Prof. **B .B . Puri,** Chairman,Research Institute of Vedic Culture; who have enlightened us with their knowledge and experience. Their moral support and cooperation was extremely valuable to us in preparation of this book.

Our friends, admirers & clients spread around the globe also helped us in compiling this book for which we are grateful to them.

We are thankful to **Er. H. Ahuja,** Vice-President, Institute of Vaastu & Joyful Living; who devoted a lot of time for material research and editing.

We are extremely obliged to **Sh. Gagan Aggarwal,** President Aadi Shankaracharya ,Vedic Education Society & **Rt. O. P. Bhardwaj,** Vice-Chairman Parampara for their inspiration and encouragement to present this book in its present form.

We are also sincerely thankful to Shri.A.J.Seghal Director Lotus Press without whose continous efforts this treatise would not have been presented to the enlightened readers in its present form.

Pracharya S. R. Jaipuria **Pt. Gopal Sharma**

CONTENTS

1

INTRODUCTION TO NUMEROLOGY

Numerology is the metaphysical science—or philosophy—of numbers asserting that every object and living being within the universe can be explained, revealed and/or reflected through numbers. It is linked to the ancient mathematicians' belief that the foundation of the entire universe is built on numbers. Not unlike the core of computer intelligence, where the entire language is a combination of the numbers zero and one, numerology analyses combinations of the numbers 1 through 9 to determine a language or science of its own.

Basically, numerology assigns a single-digit numerical value to every letter, month, day, year, etc. and then uses these numbers to predict and analyse. For instance, all the letters in your name can be translated into numbers, then added and reduced to a single-digit number that reveals your true self. Most numerologists assert that each of us has been given a unique name intended just for us that reflects our own personal spiritual vibration or essence. And in the way that your name reflects your personal vibration, your birth details reveal your destiny. Still, there are other numerologists who believe that as our names and the years change so, too, do we. Nothing is absolutely sacred or carved in stone. Whatever their personal belief, most numerologists believe very much in anything spiritual and/or divine. They promote the ideas of karma, past lives, destiny, souls, etc.

1.1. HISTORY OF NUMEROLOGY

Although the great mathematician and philosopher *Pythagorus* is considered the Father of modern numerology, numerology's history begins well before the famous Greek's irrevocable influence on our understanding of numbers. The exact date of numerology's origin may forever remain unknown despite the fact that many devotees still search the history books for clues. Hints abound in the religious doctrines of Christianity, Judaism, and Islam; it has been suggested that the answer may even be locked inside the walls of a great pyramid or Egyptian tomb we are yet to uncover. Time may or may not tell.

For the most part, numerologists recognise ancient Babylon as the earliest period of recorded history of numerology, where the *Chaldean system* of numerology was born under the influence of the Hebrews. However, with the birth of a certain Greek philosopher in 569 B.C.E., Chaldean numerology fell into a state of relative anonymity. The system is seldom used amongst numerologists and is generally unheard of by the average lay person.

Re-invigorated with the Pythagorean system, numerology has flourished, remaining largely untouched since the days of Pythagorus and enjoying worldwide recognition. Along with the practices of Feng Shui and Astrology, numerology is often used by business tycoons, entrepreneurs and spiritualists to increase their levels of success and happiness.

Numerology is perhaps the easiest of the occult arts to understand and use. All you need is the birth date and the complete name of an individual to unlock all of the secrets that the numbers hold. There are eleven numbers used in constructing Numerology charts. These numbers are 1, 2, 3, 4, 5, 6, 7, 8, 9, 11, and 22. Larger numbers that occur from adding the numbers in the complete birth date or from the values assigned to each name, are reduced by adding the digits together until the sum achieved is one of the core numbers. Merely add the components of the larger number together (repeatedly, if necessary) until a single digit (or the "master" numbers 11 or 22) results. Each of these number represents different characteristics and expressions.

Master number are the only exception to rule of reducing to the single digit. The master numbers 11 and 22 are intensified versions of the single digit number they replace (2 and 4). These numbers suggest a potential for a high degree of learning and/or achievement very often in a more stressful environment. In many individuals, the master numbers operate at a much more tangible or practical level, becoming essentially the same as the single digit parallel. Some experts consider 33 also as a 'master number' denoting super intelligence and capacity to teach even great gurus.

The first consideration of numerology is often the *date of birth*. This date, expressed numerically, as mm/dd/yyyy, is used to determine what is called the Lifepath Number and a variety of other factors in the numerology reading. We will also be converting your FULL BIRTH NAME to a number. Letters and numbers, you will learn, are always one and the same. Here is a chart of the values assigned to each of the letters in the English alphabet which is most commonly used:

1	2	3	4	5	6	7	8	9
A	B	C	D	E	F	G	H	I
J	K	L	M	N	O	P	Q	R
S	T	U	V	W	X	Y	Z	

We will compare various systems used in numerology to translate the value of letters into numerical structures and learn the general meaning of the numbers 1 through 9, 11, 22 and 33. Within the vast field of numerology, you will find different charts that display alphabets and their corresponding numbers. Although there are several, including the *Kabbalah* and the *Ulian*, there are generally only two that are used on a regular basis. As mentioned in our brief history lesson, these two systems are the *Chaldean* and *Pythagorean* conversion methods.

1.1.1. Pythagorean System

By far the most popular system found in numerology, the Pythagorean conversion chart is featured directly below. Easy to use and understand, it incorporates the numbers one to nine in its conversion system. Later on Count Louis Hemon (popularly known as Cheiro) modified and propagated this science (1-8).

1.1.2. Chaldean System

Based on the Hebrew alphabet, Chaldean numerology is another system used in numerology, albeit used much less often than the Pythagorean system. It incorporates the numbers one through eight, but is different from Cheiro.

We are giving below the table for all the three systems.

Table 1.

Alphabet	Cheiro	Cheldean/ Sepherial	Pythagoras
A	1	1	1
B	2	2	2
C	3	2	3
D	4	4	4
E	5	5	5
F	8	8	6

G	3	3	7
H	5	8	8
I	1	1	9
J	1	1	6
K	2	2	1
L	3	3	2
M	4	4	3
N	5	5	4
O	7	7	5
P	8	8	6
Q	1	1	7
R	2	2	8
S	3	3	9
T	4	4	1
U	6	6	2
V	6	6	7
W	6	6	5
X	5	6	3
Y	1	1	4
Z	7	7	5

The name number of Subhash Bose from all the three system are:

— 2 (Pythagorean)

— 3 (Chaldean/Cepherial)

— 6 (Cheiro)

You have just mastered the fundamental aspect of numerology.

1.2. MEANING OF NUMBERS

In numerology, each of the numbers one through nine has an inherent meaning that is found within its vibration. The meaning of each of the numbers is the basis of numerological analysis. Before we learn how to calculate our personal numbers, let's take a closer look at what each number symbolises or represents.

1.2.1. The Number One

The first of all numbers, The Number One is also the Leader of all numbers. People with the number one in their charts are creative, energetic, independent, and intuitive. These are the people that exude self-confidence from their every pore and silently beckon us to follow them. But even though number ones tend to be very generous, they can also become self-obsessed and insolent, deluding themselves into believing they are almighty and all-knowing.

1.2.2. The Number Two

Almost the complete opposite of the number one, The Number Two represents synergy and diplomacy. Not interested in becoming great leaders, people with the number two in their charts are content to work behind the scenes supporting and encouraging others. Gentle, sweet, supportive and loving, number twos have a tendency to allow others to walk all over them and influence their already fragile self-confidence and self-esteem. Depression and low self-confidence may become a problem for the number two.

1.2.3. The Number Three

The Number Three is exuberance incarnate. Happy-go-lucky and full of life, people with a number three in their charts are the consummate "life of the party!" Lucky, creative, and very extrovert number threes love the finer things in life, spending money as quickly as they receive it. A flirt with his or her head in the clouds, the three person has the negative tendency to become overlay critical and sharp-tongued. Their moods are also known to fluctuate.

1.2.4. The Number Four

The Number Four represents pragmatism, security and stability. A hard worker with a practical mind geared toward the future, a person with number four as the total of his name, alphabets or date of birth is the purest "head of the family" who looks after those he or she cares about. The number four's strengths are its steadfastness and tenacity; its weaknesses, rigidity and lifelessness. Along with that streak of practicality comes the tendency to be a bit of a bore.

1.2.5. The Number Five

The Number Five symbolises change, rebellion, and freedom. People with the number five or (14, 23) as their name or birth number (D.O.B) value freedom above all else, often times rebelling against the *status quo,* going where no one has dared go before, and refusing to allow others to dictate any control over them. Number fives often have trouble with commitment and can be talented at many things, but specialised in none. Because of this lack of commitment, people with the number five can begin to feel overwhelmed, having started many projects but finishing none.

1.2.6. The Number Six

The Number Six represents the home, family, love, beauty and romance. People with the number six as their D.O.B or name number or destiny number or even Kua number (Chinease system) are very loving, kind, and gentle. They are affectionate and tender and are natural born parents. And yet, since most of their decisions come from their heart it may be impossible to reach these soul creatures with reason. Add to this their unrelenting and fixed natures, and they can become difficult to live with, possibly even leaving the nest if they feel the love is no longer deep enough to sustain them.

1.2.7. The Number Seven

The Number Seven is often seen as the most eccentric of all the numbers. Mystical, deep, analytical, wise and intuitive, people with the number seven in their chart are the quintessential loners who seemingly abandon society in exchange for their own personal quests of knowledge and wisdom. But the number seven has many gifts and talents to share with the world and often makes a wonderful teacher. The number seven can become a bit out of touch with the needs of others if they withdraw too much; thus a balance should be sought.

1.2.8. The Number Eight

The Number Eight is one of the most powerful numbers in numerology. People with the number eight in their charts are born for achievement, success and leadership. They thrive on rising through a hierarchal organisation and manipulating those working alongside them to become part of their own vessel. They love money and grandeur and may stop at nothing to achieve their desired success. These people are best bankers, criminal lawyers or financial controllers and normally prefer to study B.Com, C.A., Law or Automobile/Mechanical Engineering.

1.2.9. The Number Nine

As the number one is the beginning of all things, the Number Nine is the end. It represents humanitarianism, compassion, tolerance and both spiritual and material success. People with the number nine in their charts are idealistic mystics that long to leave the world a better place. They are blessed with more charm and compassion than all of the numbers added together. Unfortunately, they can become too idealistic, forcing their beliefs onto others and/or becoming prejudiced against those who do not follow the path they themselves have chosen.

1.3. THE MASTER NUMBERS

In addition to the numbers one through nine, there are numbers that numerologists refer to as master numbers. These numbers are 11, 22, 33, 44, 55, 66, 77, 88; and 99. It is said that the master numbers operate at a much higher vibration than the numbers one through nine, and that they also include the vibration of their single-digit reduction. For instance, the master number eleven would be written as 11/2, and consequently carries both the vibrations for eleven and two. People with a master number as their destiny number are called upon to bring many great gifts to the world.

1.3.1. The Number Eleven (11/2)

The Number Eleven represents spiritual truth and communication. People with a number eleven in their charts are often highly intuitive and have a great message to share with the world. However, they may never be heard unless they can overcome their impulsivity and tendency to transpose their faults onto others.

Example of Destiny No. 11

Find Destiny No. of a person born on

January 18th 1990.

We constrict a sum from his date of birth

(M)	(D)	(Y)
01	18	1990
		01 (M)
		18 (D)
		1+9+9+0 (Y)
		1+9+1 =11

This person has a *Destiny No.* **11**

1.3.2. The Number Twenty-Two(22/4)

Whereas the master number eleven has a message to convey to the world, the Number Twenty-two has come back to build something. People with the number twenty-two in their charts long to leave something grand and everlasting behind them that will hope-fully remain standing long after they have gone. They have an amazing ability to turn dreams into reality. However, twenty-twos can be very sensitive, falling victim to the demands placed upon them by others and becoming generally overwhelmed, failing to complete their dream.

Example of Destiny No. 22

Find Destiny No of a person born on

November 4th 1960.

We constrict a sum from his date of birth

(M)	(D)	(Y)
11	4	1960
		11 (M)
		04 (D)
		1+9+6+0 (Y)
		2+4+16 = 22

This person has a *Destiny No.*

22

1.3.3. The Number Thirty Three (33/6)

The 33 is the most influential of all numbers. It is the Master of Healing Love. The 33 combines the 11 and the 22 and brings their potential to another level. When expressed to the fullest, the 33 lacks all personal ambition and instead focuses its considerable abilities toward the spiritual uplifting of

Example of Destiny No. 33

Find Destiny No of a person born on

July 9th 1961

We constrict a sum from his date of birth

(M)	(D)	(Y)
07	06	1961
		7 (M)
		6 (D)
		1+9+6+1 (Y)
		2+4+17 = 33

This person has a *Destiny No.*

33

mankind. What makes the 33 especially impressive, is the high level of sincere devotion. This is shown in its determination to seek understanding and wisdom before preaching to others. The 33 in full force is extremely rare. The 33 is on the journey of discovering its powerful healing energy through an open heart and unconditional love.

2

VEDIC NUMEROLOGY

Astronomy, mathematics, astrology, numerology, logic, philosophy, gemology etc., all derive from the mighty encyclopaedia called *Vedas*. Astronomy, mathematics and numerology evolved from the wisdom of the heavens, astrology. Astrology, the science of time was revealed to our ancient research scholars (sages) in yogic flashes of heightened consciousness. Astro-numerology was the perfect blend of the science of the numbers and the science of time.

Vedas are not only holy books of Hindus. These are the celestial truths cognised by *seers* (research scholars) in higher states of consciousness. These scientific and philosophic truths were written down by their devoted disciples and called *Vedas*. They can be cognised by anyone who cultivate the same spiritual discipline; irrespective of religion, community, caste or creed.

Vedic numerology, the perfect unification between the science of numbers and the wisdom of the heavens was initiated in the West by Pythagoras and by Vararuchi in the East. To Pythagorus the mystery of the Universe was inter-comprehensible in the notion of the number. The letters *0 to 9* are numbers and infinity was defined as a numberless number. Philosophically, when we say everything is unity, we are talking about numbers or that "Infinity is the beginning of all things."

Pythagorus, the great mathematician who discovered 'PI' (π), also discovered the law of vibration. This law states that each number has a particular vibration. Astro-numerology is the synthesis of astrology and numerology, the perfect integration between the science of the heavens and the science of numbers!

1. One represents the luminary	**SUN**
2. Two represents the luminary	**MOON**
3. Three represents the planet	**JUPITER**
4. Four represents the planet	**RAHU**
5. Five represents the planet	**MERCURY**
6. Six represents the planet	**VENUS**
7. Seven represents the planet	**KETU**
8. Eight represents the planet	**SATURN**
9. Nine represents the planet	**MARS**

Ketu and Rahu are the Nodes of the Moon. The Moon's Ascending Node is Rahu and the Descending Node is Ketu. The orbit of the Sun and the Moon intersect at two points and they are these Nodes.

2.1. ONE—LUMINARY SUN

This number is the middle and the centre of all numbers. This number represents all that is created and the visible Actuality. Individuals born under this number aspire for greatness in no uncertain way. Basically creative and imaginative people having great originality and individuality people born under this number are determined and engaged in noble activities.

These qualities will exist in no uncertain degree in those who are born on dates 1, 10, 19, 28, etc. These qualities will be highly manifest in those born in the month when the Sun is in the highest exalted position. (From March 21 to April 28). Persons born under this number always rise high in their respective professions. To achieve the *summum bonum*, the highest *altaltissimo* in their profession, is their main objective. Whatever be their field, they always protect their authority and the wishes of their subordinates.

They always use their days (1, 10, 19, 28) for the implementation of their creative plans. They are very friendly with people whose numbers are 2, 3, 5 and 9. The most auspicious days are Sunday and Monday. If the numbers 3, 5, and 9 coincides with these days that days work will be highly fruitful.

Alexander the Great, Emperor Paul of Russia, Indira Gandhi, Saddam Hussain, Bill Clinton, Dhirubhai Ambani, were born under the influence of number one.

It is the most powerful luminary in intrinsic strength. It is one of the functional luminaries and is the King in the Government of the Almighty. Hence all regal qualities are attributed to this luminary.

2.1.1.Unitarian

You are interested in the psychic sciences. You are more active than contemplative. You are regal in outlook and always adopt a pragmatic approach to life. You are more practical than sentimental.

You may be not successful in the worldly sphere as you are not much attached to wealth and possessions. You are not much careful about spending.

You are frank and outspoken. Because of that you generate many secret enemies. But they will always dread you because of your inherent fine qualities.

The Sun represents Prudence the greatest of all the seven cardinal virtues. This quality will be predominant in you. As this virtue predominates in you people will honour and respect you even during adversity.

The zodiac sign representing this number is Leo. People born under this zodiacal constellation are truly leonine and overactive. Regal in outlook and adventurous in nature, Leoninians always push their way to the top. If the Sun is strongly positioned in their horoscopes they will definitely get chances to exhibit their regal valour.

People consider you rash and ambitious. The Sun represents Politics, the science of the state. The Solarians are usually politically conscious and politically oriented. If these people are born in between March 21 to April 28 (viz- when the Sun is in a state of deep exaltation) their shining in political field will become a living reality.

You can expect political victory when the Sun transits favourable points like March 21 to April 28 and August 16 to Sept 16. Your main drawback is that you jump into things without much aforethought. You should learn to persevere rather than quit. *Patience is another virtue which you should incorporate.*

Regarding diseases, the most likely disease which may affect the Solarians is the disease of the heart. Blood pressure is also another. Eye troubles are also indicated. Their best fruits and medicinal leaves are dried grapes, nutmeg, orange, lemon, and ginger. They should take in honey. They should take care of their health at the ages 19, 28, 37, 55 & 64. They should guard against ill health and excess exercise during the months of October, December and January.

The Solarians are prone to sudden anger. Anger is said to be man's greatest enemy. Sun is considered to be a natural malefic in Astrology. You may indulge in politics and its negative aspect manifests as lack of mental peace and happiness.

Like Pythagoras' intoxication with the Music of the Spheres(Wisdom), the Indian Sages were infatuated with Knowledge. Many scientific truths were cognised by them in higher states of consciousness which came to be known as the *Vedas*. One such sage was Vararuchi, who discovered the interrelationship between numbers and letters of the alphabet.

2.1.2. Name Number

It is the total of all the numbers given to the letters of the alphabet as per the system of Cheiro (1-9).

Individual name number: The name number is arrived by adding all the digits which correspond to the letters in his name. For example:

M A N	M O H A N	S I N G H
4 + 1 + 5	4 + 7 + 5 + 1 + 5	3 + 1 + 5 + 3 + 5

= 10 + 22 + 17
= 1 + 4 + 8
= 1 + 3
= 4

Here the individual name number is 4 and the combined name number is 49. There are effects for both the individual and the combined name numbers in vedic numerology.

2.2. TWO—LUMINARY MOON

Moon is considered very important in Vedic Sidereal Astrology. Mental strength depends on the strength of the Moon in one's natal chart.

2.2.1. Twoian

You are ruled numerologically by the luminary Moon.

The main characteristic of Moon is its fickle and inconstant nature and this can sway your temperament. You are moody at times and this depression generally saps your vitality.

The best remedy for you is to take recourse to yogic practices to overcome depression. Have implicit faith in God. Optimism is far better than pessimism.

Your inconstant nature makes you hesitant at times. You may lack self-assertion and become indecisive at times.

If you wear a ring studded with Moonstone you can overcome the negative vibrations of this number. This ring should be worn on Monday of the bright fortnight after dedicating yourself to the Lord.

Lunarians are generally timid and accommodative. Hence they are sentimental and oversensitive. Heavenly topics interest you a great deal. You show inclination towards Astrology and other allied sciences.

Wealthwise you are subject to terrific ups and downs corresponding to the lunar phases of waxing and waning. You will be subject to emotional suffering. You like to travel. Your honesty will be appreciated by people.

Your personal magnetism will win friends and influence people. Your special charm will offset the minus-points caused by the fickle and inconstant nature of the Moon.

Mental strength and courage will be adversely affected at times. The ideal remedial measure will be to fast on Mondays devoting yourself to the Mother Divine.

In Vedic Astrology, Moon rules the mind. If you consider Chankya's statement "An irrational or a controlled mind can make a hell out of heaven or a heaven out of hell" you can visualise how important the luminary Moon is. The *Vedas* reveal that Moon represents the mind of the Cosmic Man (*Chandrama manaso Jatha*) and is one of the important political planets. Their fortunate dates are 2, 11, 20 and 29 and auspicious days are Monday, Tuesday and Sunday. If both of these combine, best are the results. People born on these dates are friendly with those having numbers 7 and 9. M.K. Gandhi, Morarji Desai, Harshad Mehta, Dilip Kumar, Shah Rukh Khan and Rajesh Khanna are born under this influence.

2.2.2. Zodiac Sign—Cancer

The zodiac sign representing this number is Cancer. Cancer represents the heart of the Cosmic Man and Cancerians are tied and tuned to the cosmic world. Cancerians are generally adaptive to any conditions. *Soft heartedness is the bane of the Cancerian.*

Resilience is the major forte of the Cancerian. He can struggle against adversity and challenge with an intrepidity which can surprise anyone. Cancerians are generally home-loving . Love of the fine arts, music, dance and cinema are their main inclinations. Diseases of the stomach may affect them during middle age . In order to alleviate the suffering watery fruits and herbal medicines may be taken.

In Vedic gemology, Moon represents Pearl or Moonstone. Wearing this stone on a Shukla Paksha Monday (fifteen days after the New Moon) will enhance the luck of the Twoians. The Sanskrit text T*he Jataka Chandrika* assigns Pearl to the Moon (*Vimalam Muktaphalam Sheetagau*) Monday is the day of the Moon (from the Latin dies Luna and the Sanskrit Somavar).

2.3. THREE—THE PLANET JUPITER

Three—ruled by the Divine Minister of the Solar Logos,

Jupiter. *Jupiter is considered to be a supreme benefic in Astrology*. He is so large and voluminous that 1300 earths can be fit into him. If well posited in a quadrant in one's natal chart, he can give divine protection to the native.

2.3.1. Threeian

Your Numerological Number is 3 and your Life Controller is the divine planet Jupiter. This wisdom planet has all to do with trinities and trilogies. They are very friendly with 6 and 9.

They always aspire for greatness as they can never be satisfied with working under a shadow. They want to control others. They are stern and immaculate in the implementation of their duties and responsibilities. They love discipline. *They obey the law and make others obey the law*. The Jupiterians always rise high in Navy Army and administration. As they implement their duties religiously they shine in almost all realms where sincerity and responsibility are called for.

Their drawback is that as they are devoted to the Law they force their ideals on others. Even though they are not quarrelsome they create a lot of enemies. They are proud and vain- glorious. They will not serve others. They are annoyed at the slightest adversity. They should use 3, 12, 21 and 30 for the fructification of their efforts.

Their fortunate days are Thursday and Tuesday. If these days coincide with 3, 12, 21, 30, 6, 9, 15, 18, 24, 27 these dates become fortunate. They are very friendly with 6 and 9. Shakespeare, Winston Churchill, Benazir Bhutto, Ma Nirmala Devi, Sharad Pawar and Shammi Kapoor were born under this number.

Vedic numerology, the perfect synthesis between astrology and numerology deals with the correspondence between the nine revolving heavens and the nine numbers. It also deals with the effect of many Numbers-the Fadic Number, the Name Number and the Birth Number and the combined Fadic, Name and Birth Numbers. The Pythagorean Law of Vibration states that each number has a particular vibration.

2.4. FOUR—THE PLANET RAHU

In astronomy, the two mathematical points where the orbits of the Moon and the Sun intersect are called Ascending Node (North Node) and Descending Node (South Node), Rahu and Ketu. (The orbits of the Sun and the Moon differ by 8 degrees). They are not actual planets but are shadowy planets. They are important determinants of behaviour. In Sidereal Astrology great importance is attached to the Nodal Axis which becomes the pivot of the horoscope. In Mythology (which is allegorical and symbolic), Rahu and Ketu are characterised as demons as both these shadowy planets are natural malefics. Rahu resembles Saturn and Ketu, Mars.

2.4.1. Fourian

Your Numerological Number is 4 ruled by the Moon's Ascending Node, Rahu. The character of the Fourians is unique and known only to themselves. They view all things from a totally different angle as opposed to the ordinary people who view everything from a common angle. In every argument they argue from the opposite side and because of this tendency they gain a lot of secret enemies. They hate all laws and legal frameworks & destroy all such laws.

They oppose the rulers and always establish their own kingdoms and republics. *They always believe in the freedom of expression and opinion.* People who are born on 4, 13, 22 and 31 do not make friends easily. People with numbers 7 and 8 attract them. Some scholars believe that people with numbers 1 and 2 also have a hidden attractions for them. The Fourians do not succeed in the realm of material prosperity like the others. If they save money or make money the way they use it will astound everybody. From June 21 to July 21 and July 22 to the end of August is the best time for the fructification of their efforts. Their lucky days are Saturday, Sunday, Monday. If these days coincide with the 4, 13, 22, 31, 1, 2, 7, 10, 11, 16, 19, 20, 25, 28, 29 these days will be the most auspicious. Their main drawbacks are that they are loners separated from this world often living in desperation and silence.

Your lucky day	Saturday
Your lucky month	April
Your lucky dates	4, 13, 22 and 31
Your lucky colour	Black

George Washington, Lord Byron, Margarat Thatcher, Kishore Kumar, Swami Ram Tirath and Munshi Prem Chand were born under this number.

When the revealed science of the heavens and the science of numbers merge, we have a lovely resultant science, vedic numerology. The great Paracelsus averred that the knowledge of the mysteries of the Universe must be utilised for the welfare of mankind as these sciences play an important role in our lives—for they are pointers to the ultimate reality.

2.5. FIVE—THE PLANET MERCURY

2.5.1. Fivian

Your numerological number is 5 and Your Life Controller is Mercury. The basic nature of this planet is frailty and in- constancy. In fact the word mercurial is derived from it. Despite their inconstancy they are intelligent and shrewd and they jump into fields where they can make easy money hating the hazardous and the laborious paths. They take decisions quickly without much aforethought. They are very greedy merchants and involved in stockmarket dealings. They have remarkable resilience.

No crisis can shake them. Their lucky days are Wednesday and Friday. The best days they should select for their efforts are 5 14 23. Their main drawback is that they use all their creative energy and becomes subject to nervous complaints. They are irate to a fault and cannot face failure.

Netaji Subhash Chandra Bose, Jawahar Lal Nehru, Albert Einstein, Prince of Wales, Murli Manohar Joshi and Kumar Mangalam Birla were born under this number.

2.6. SIX—THE PLANET VENUS

2.6.1. Sixian

Your numerological number is 6 and you are ruled by the fair planet, Venus. Venus represents the aesthetic element and hence your tendencies will be towards drama, music & cinema poetry and the arts. Venus represents the poet and philosopher. Venusians love material life and the pleasures of the mundane. Venus is defined as "the fair planet that hearteneth to love" by Dante. Attractive to the other sex, you will be endowed with personal magnetism.

As you are under the sway of Venus, the arts will have a tremendous influence on you. Poetry will flourish under your guidance. You are temperamental and moody at times. Venusians are generally gentle and persevering people. Your ability to talk your way through and influence people will pay large rewards as many people will be influenced by you. The personal magnetism which you generate will be felt by one and all. Your best and lucky day is Friday. Venus is known as Freya in Norse Mythology and Freya's day became Friday. Friday was consecrated to Venus.

When the celestial science of the Heavens blends with the science of Numbers, we have the fascinating Vedic Numerology. While Pythagorus initiated Numerology in the West, Astrology was initiated by eighteen Seers from India. They were the seer-poets who composed the *Vedas*, scriptures which were never written and which were cognised in higher states of Consciousness. The best days are 6, 15, 24. A.P.J. Abdul Kalam, Dalai Lama, Madhuri Dixit, George Bush, Jai Lalitha and Maharshi Arvind are born under this number.

2.7. SEVEN—THE PLANET KETU

The two mathematical points where the orbits of the Moon and the Sun intersect are called Ascending Node (North Node) and Descending Node (South Node), Rahu and Ketu. (The orbits of the Sun and the Moon differ by 8 degrees). They are shadowy planets and not actual planets. They are important determinants of behaviour. In Vedic Astrology great importance is attached to the Nodal Axis which becomes the pivot of the horoscope.

In Mythology (which is allegorical and symbolic), Rahu and Ketu are characterised as demons as both these shadowy planets are natural malefics. Rahu resembles Saturn and Ketu, Mars.

2.7.1. Sevenian

Your Numerological Number is 7 and your Life Controller is Ketu. This is the number of those born on the 7 16 and the 25th of every month. They are very friendly with the Lunarians — that is people born on the 2 11 20 29. They are very independent prominent and with great individuality. As they are restless they love travel and change. They love travel particularly in foreign countries.

They are not lucky in financial matters. But women born under this number are always anxious about their own future and always find out nice matrimonial alliances. They are rich in ideas which will find their way to fulfilment. Their thoughts are noble. They gain a lot of knowledge about the sea and try to establish business ties with foreign countries.

About religion their ideas are different. They try to found new innovative and creative religions. They always dream wonderful dreams. They love occult sciences. They are always intuitive. To gain the fructifiction of their objectives they should use 7 16 and 25. Their lucky days are Sunday and Monday. Ravidra Nath Tagore, Charles Dickens, Oscar Wilde, Hema Malini, Atal Behari Vajpai and Charlie Chaplin were born under the influence of this number.

2.8. EIGHT—THE PLANET SATURN

2.8.1. Eigthian

Your numerological number is 8 and your life controller is Saturn. People often misunderstand them and because of that they suffer mentally and become loners. They are people with great individuality and depth in learning. If religious they will take to religion in a great manner. In order to win arguments they destroy the opposition verbally and create a lot of secret enemies.

They have great sympathy for the oppressed and show a lot of laziness and lack of enthusiasm. They are extremists; that is they are either very successful or great failures. People under the influence of this number normally have to bear great ills, losses and humiliations. The ancient Greeks called this number the number of justice. There is no middle course for them. These people always aspire for greatness, strive for leadership and sacrifice their personal comforts to maintain the high posts earned by them as a result of their laborious endeavours. Anyway 8 is not a lucky number.

Their best days are 8, 17 and 26. If 4, 13, 22, 31 coincide with Saturday Sunday and Monday these days become very auspicious Their best jewel is Blue Sapphire. It is very good for them if they wear this stone. The number 8 is made up of two circles and is the sum of 2 4's. This was considered to be the great decision of Universal Law which rules races and individuals. Saturn is also known as the Planet of Destiny. It has relevance to both material and spiritual aspects of Life.

Revolution, anarchy, earthquakes and all sorts of evil and uncommon events are represented by this number. On the other hand philosophy, religious fervour, One-pointedness of mind, determination — all these are also represented by this number. They feel that they are different from the rest and therefore unique. They lack happiness. They also fail to reap the good actions they have done in this life. But even then they are admired after a long time.

George Bernard Shaw, Jyoti Basu, Dr. B.V. Raman, Dr. Man Mohan Singh, Lal Krishna Advani and Dev Anand were born like you under this number and it will not be surprising if anyone identifies similar characteristics in you.

2.9. NINE—THE PLANET MARS

Your Fadic Number is 9 and your Life Controller is the

planet of War, Mars. This is the number of those born under the 9th 18th and 27th of every month. They are born fighters in all aspects of Life. Even though they are faced by adversity, they emerge victorious in the end because of their mental strength, determination and courage. They are arbitrarians and never become slaves to anybody. If the number 9 occurs in their major events they create big enemies and generate quarrels and enmity.

They always suffer bruises either financially or in the battlefield. They are highly courageous and become great soldiers. Their love of themselves that is their arbitrarianism is the major cause of their adversity. They are prone to accidents resulting from fire. They always quarrel with their friends and in-laws. They do not like advice. They love to be revered as big in their domestic life. As they are capable of forming organisations if they do not get the leadership they become the cause of destroying the organisations.

Loving women can make monkeys of them as they will do anything for their beloved. They are friendly with 3 6 and 9. They are very compatible with 9. This number has a lot of peculiarities. Any number into 9 will yield 9. Red confers luck on them. Their best days are Thursday, Tuesday and Friday. They should use 9, 18 and 27 for the fructification of their objectives. If the above mentioned days coincide with 3, 6,12,15, 21, 24, 30 these days become very auspicious for them.

In psychic sciences great importance have been attached to the numbers 7 and 9. While 7 represents the underlying Divine Unity, 9 represents the physical and the material. President Roosevelt, Kiran Bedi, Chaitanya Maha Prabhu, Mahesh Yogi and Sonia Gandhi were born under this number and it will not be surprising if people identify similar characteristics in them.

2.10. AUSPICIOUS AND INAUSPICIOUS MONTHS FOR DIFFERENT NUMBERS

Table below gives chart of auspicious and inauspicious months for each number.

Table 1. Auspicious and inauspicious months for each number

Number	Inauspicious month	Auspicious month
1	May-June	April-August
2	May-August	July-September
3	April-August	June-September
4	March-May-December	January-August-October
5	February-April-November	March-September
6	January-August-October	March-September-December
7	January-September-October	February-June-November
8	March-June-December	January-April-October
8	January-July-October	March-June

3

THE LIFE PATH NUMBER

Of all the numbers found in numerology, none is hailed as highly as the "Life Path Number." This single digit number is considered by the average person to be the whole of numerological theory.

Of all the numbers used by numerologists, the Life Path Number is often considered the most important, the crowning glory of all the other numbers. Found from our birth dates it is unchangeable and so governs our destiny forever. Specifically, the Life Path Number tells us the lessons we need to learn in this lifetime and then shows each of us the talents we possess that will help us to learn these lessons. Numerologists believe that we will constantly be tested by the universe until we learn these lessons, experiencing many similar situations that call on us to overcome our shortcomings and attain a sort of enlightenment.

Enlightenment—in numerology—means that you attain an actualisation of your higher self in which you become a better, more content and complete person. But, if somewhere along the way you also contact your divine self, fabulous!! The Life Path Number, then, highlights the "paths" our lives will follow, revealing where we will find our true successes, even our failures. It is also sometimes called the Destiny Number.

3.1. CALCULATING THE LIFE PATH NUMBER

In order to calculate the Life Path Number all you will need to know is your date of birth. You do not need to know the time you were born, whether or not the moon was full that particular day, or which planets were squaring the planet the exact minute you were born. The simplest way to demonstrate how to calculate the Life Path Number is to give you an example. We can use a birth date to do so.

Birth Date = February 26, 1975

The first step in calculating the Life Path Number is to convert all of the birth date into a numerical value. Therefore, the month in which we were born must also be translated into a number. Most of us are familiar with the numbers of each month, but just in case you are not familiar with this system.

January	=	1
February	=	2
March	=	3
April	=	4
May	=	5
June	=	6
July	=	7
August	=	8
September	=	9
October	=	10(1)
November	=	11(2)
December	=	12(3)

It is important to note that if you were born in either the month of October, November or December you must reduce your birth month to a single digit. For instance December = 12, but in numerology we would need to reduce that number to a single digit. We would do this by adding the 1 and 2 to get a 3 (i.e. December = 12 = 1 + 2 = 3).

February 26, 1975 becomes 02 26, 1975. We then add up all the numbers.

2+2+6+1+9+7+5

=32

=3+2

=5

The Life Path Number, then, is the number 5. We will separate each of the elements of our birth dates. You can add up your day of birth, month of birth, and year of birth and then add them together.

For example.

February 26, 1975

=2 + (2+6) + (1+9+7+5)

=2+8+(22)

=2+8+(2+2)

=2+8+4

=14

=5

When calculating the Life Path Number, yes, we want to reduce it to a single digit. But, the double-digit number also holds information from our past and the lessons we need to learn. Henceforth, the Life Path Number would be written as follows:

Life Path Number = 14/5

For another example.

Birth Date = April 25, 1975

= 4 + (2 + 5) + (1 + 9 + 7 + 5)

= 4 + 7 + (22)

= 4 + 7 + (2 + 2)

= 4 + 7 + 4

= 15

= 6

This person's Life Path Number would then be 15/6. Now that we know how to calculate the Life Path Number, let's discover exactly what this numerological number has to say about each of us. Related to each number's strengths and weaknesses, the Life Path Numbers encourage us to perfect our imperfect selves.

3.1.1. Life Path Number One

Your life path will take you to the heights of independence and leadership. But before you can attain your destined success, you must learn to practise moderation, develop patience and accept your limitations. You must also resign yourself to the fact that the world does not revolve around you.

3.1.2. Life Path Number Two

Your life path is one of harmony, teamwork and co-operation; you are destined to unite people in common good. But in order to succeed in your life path you will need to learn to say "no," refusing to allow others to take advantage of your generosity and gentility. You also need to get your head out of the clouds - too much fantasy could keep you from actualising your goals.

3.1.3. Life Path Number Three

Your life path is one of exuberance, spontaneity, joy and inspiration. However, you must learn reliability and responsibility, growing to respect others through honesty and kindness. In other words, try and curb that blunt tongue of yours!

3.1.4. Life Path Number Four

Your life path will be marked by hard work and steadfastness, laying down strong foundations and building a steady future. With your 4 Life Path Number you will need to learn to accept change, however, refusing to dwell in "what was" and may never be again. Try to take life a little less seriously and remember that it may be better to be kind and loved rather than strict and righteous.

3.1.5. Life Path Number Five

Your life path is sure to be defined with change, rebellion, and freedom. But if you are to ever truly enjoy your desired freedom you must learn personal discipline in achieving a high level of commitment to one ideal, dream, and/or goal. You are in danger of floundering through life jumping from job to job, passion to passion, and relationship to relationship without achieving any real success.

3.1.6. Life Path Number Six

Your life path is trying to teach you about harmony and responsibility and the balance between work and home. You need to learn all of these above qualities and priorities, growing to understand your own cycles of mood, enthusiasm, creativity and ability. Get in touch with your own sense of self and harmony and use it! This doesn't mean that you must be a single-faced docile creature, for as a number 6 you have many sides to your nature. But, you still MUST learn harmony, synergy, tranquility, and responsibility if you are ever to find your life's true success.

3.1.7. Life Path Number Seven

Your life path is the path of the explorer and wisdom seeker who instinctively understands the subtle intricacies and spiritual truths of life. But your sensitivity often leaves you feeling overwhelmed and if you are to achieve your life path's success you need to sit down and truly ponder your goals and desires in life. You need to remove yourself from the tedious and overwhelming demands of your daily activities and seek the divine.

3.1.8. Life Path Number Eight

Your life path will be one of authority, mastery and dominance. But you are in danger of valuing money and material worth over the inherent value of life and beauty. You must learn to accept others as they are - splendid in all of their different skins and coats - ensuring that you don't begin to hail conformity above individuality. Before you can find your life path's truest measure of success, you will need to master justice and compassion.

3.1.9. Life Path Number Nine

The life path of the number 9 is one of great love and compassion, leading you to an unconditional acceptance of all humankind. Before you are able to give this of yourself, however, you will need to begin looking beyond yourself and developing a kinship with and love for others, learning to accept that their path in life may not be the same as yours and that perhaps that just might be okay.

3.1.10. Life Path Number Eleven

Your life path will lead you to spiritually motivate and inspire the entire breadth of humanity. You are destined to be a great leader but if you are ever to truly succeed you must learn to finish what you start, stay centered and stop transposing your own faults onto those around you. You may be in danger of losing yourself to irrational fears, imaginary limitations and a misery caused all on your own.

3.1.11. Life Path Number Twenty-Two

Your life path is to be one of life's great creators. You will help build the growing foundation of our world and universe by using your incredible organisational skills and humanitarian ideals. But, as with all master numbers, you must learn to stay centered and balanced. You are in great danger of becoming cynical and may destroy all that you build before the world ever reaps its award and/or glory. You must learn to have faith, both in yourself and in those around you.

4

THE NAME NUMBERS

In this chapter we will delve into the meaning of our names, learning how to discover our true characters through the calculation of both our given and surnames. Calculating the name numbers is very simple; we just translate each letter into a number, add up the numbers and reduce them to a single digit. It is also called as the the Expression Number.

The Expression Number (also called the Destiny Number) is the total sum of every letter of your full name, which, incidentally, is the name found on your birth certificate. Second in importance to the Life Path Number, your Expression Number reveals your truest self. This is the essence of who you are.

4.1. EXPRESSION NUMBERS

4.1.1. The Number One

You know exactly who you are, what you believe and where you are headed. You don't want to be the pencil pusher; you want to envision the pencil that will change the world, initiate its design and marketing concept, become head of the company, receive national praise and when that's done you want to move on and create something else. You are a Number One. You can be very generous and typically enjoy the company of others, displaying a genuine interest in their well being (albeit never as much as in your own). But you also have the tendency to need constant ego stroking and recognition, without which you may become aggressive or hostile.

4.1.2. The Number Two

You are a gentle, timid creature who symbolizes the classic angel without wings who helps everyone else learn how to fly. You despise conflict and disharmony and are very sensitive to other people's opinions of you. You love to fall in love, be in love, and be loved-but in a very gentle and tender way. Because of your shyness, sensitivity, and otherworld qualities, others may find you disconcerting, which can lead you to experience loneliness and depression. Generally speaking, you are a very gentle soul. Be careful that you don't give in to your negative side. Very few can be as critical or malicious as a number two scorned.

4.1.3. The Number Three

No one loves a good party like you do! Energetic, exuberant and full of life, you enjoy anything that comes your way. If something is not fun, you make sure it becomes fun. You are the consummate kid who never grew up, playing games and telling jokes long after your hair turns grey. You say exactly what is on your mind, at times crossing over the thin line between honesty and brusqueness. You enjoy the finer things in life. Brand name stereo systems and designer clothes are a must in your opinion and you have enough luck with money to somehow pull off your extravagant lifestyle. Regardless of all your great qualities, however, you can be self-centered, rude, an incessant talker, critical and unfaithful. There is no halfway for a number three.

4.1.4. The Number Four

The least exciting of all the numbers, you are defined by your sense of duty, practicality and honesty. You bring order from chaos and provide security to those around you. You finish everything that you start and work very hard at achieving your goals and establishing order. The price you pay for your efforts can be a lack of true joy, extreme depression and a general sense of gloominess. Your need for order and discipline is probably both your best and worst quality.

4.1.5. The Number Five

You are the fearless adventurer who takes life by the horns and rides it wherever it may take you. You are a natural born rebel, defying the status quo and rejecting any sense of conformity others attempt to saddle you with. You are adaptable and even enjoy change (IMAGINE that!!). You are a liberal minded and progressive person who was probably a hippie in the sixties and seventies. If you weren't around back then, you probably wish you could have been. Your natural inclination towards freedom, however, can have its drawbacks. You find any kind of commitment too difficult to manage, make hasty and impulsive decisions, and become restless if you are not living some grand adventure. Your healthy sexual appetite and attraction for the opposite sex can turn into insatiable lust and/or addictions of all kinds.

4.1.6. The Number Six

A natural born counsellor, you are the person we turn to when we need a good, strong shoulder to cry on. You are the consummate caregiver and parent. Your home and family are the most important things in your life. You are quick to put any problems right at home-disharmony in your home is very troublesome to you. You have high romantic expectations of your partner.

Your ideas of love border on delusional-sunshine, roses, walks in the moonlight, and candlelight dinners for the rest of your life seem completely practical and natural to you. Love is your ultimate desire. Love is the expression of your soul. But when others let you down you hold on to past hurts forever, dwelling in little things than cannot be undone and that you just will not forgive. And once your mind is made up, it's made up-reason and common sense are no match for you resolution.

4.1.7. The Number Seven

You are the quiet and contemplative soul that lives alone in your own mind. You seem out of touch with the rest of the world and yet that is just your way of observing everything around you. You can sit in a chair for hours whether you are reading a book, thinking about your future, daydreaming, or just staring at nothing as if lost in space. You are quite content spending your time doing "nothing."

But rarely are you doing "nothing"; you are analyzing, discovering, conceiving ideas and thoughts, even if it is just in your own mind. You are the mystic who was born old and wise. You can be quite charming and often display a dry sense of humour. Tempered with your usually high level of education and scholarly/intelligent persona, people can find you easy to be with without feeling insecure about their lesser achievements. It is people you must learn to connect with. If you spend too much time alone you can become reserved, critical, moody and distant.

4.1.8. The Number Eight

You were born for great achievement and success. You are the quintessential C.E.O., V.I.P., or Chairperson of the Board. You govern every aspect of your life with efficiency and skill. You are capable, competent and self-actualizing. You have a strong desire for material wealth and splendour and may become unscrupulous in your business dealings in order to attain your desired level of success. You show an interest in the metaphysical sciences, demonstrate a good dose of integrity (that may come and go if necessary, however), and accept others for who they are. In fact, you have a natural talent for convincing others to join your team, aiding you in achieving your goals. Number eights are not above a little good old-fashioned manipulation.

4.1.9. The Number Nine

You are a great humanitarian. You are a highly spiritual being who understands the flows of life-good and bad, up and down. Lucky, idealistic, creative and compassionate you are a parent to everyone you meet. You are a very sensitive creature who longs to reach all of humanity and change the world in some small-or tremendous-way. Your high ideals, however, can lead to a sort of high-handedness with regard to your choices and the choices of others. You may become critical of others' life choices and/or beliefs, take dis-agreements too personally and suffer from drastic high-low swings in your mood.

4.2. MASTER EXPRESSION NUMBERS

4.2.1. The Number Eleven (11/2)

You are probably psychic or have psychic abilities. You

are a rare spiritual being with a strong inclination toward the metaphysical. You enjoy all that life has to offer, fully giving yourself to every new possibility that presents itself. This may lead to a sense of emptiness, however, if you are not achieving any real sense of meaning or purpose. For you love to have your palms read, numerology charts done, etc. in hopes of discovering all there is to know about yourself. But, if you do not acknowledge your faults you may self-destruct into a self-imprisoned world of irrational doubts and fears.

4.2.2. The Number Twenty-Two (22/4)

You are a builder. You build solid relationships, interesting and productive careers, and loving and stable homes. Like the number nine, you have a strong humanitarian streak and long to make the world a better place.

You have a remarkable ability to understand the motives behind most of our behaviours and an instinctive understanding of the human condition. Because of this, you may become cynical, seeing people as all evil or all good, unable to realize that there are many shades of grey between black and white. Your hard work, however, if seasoned with patience and balance will inevitably pay off.

4.2.3. The Number Thirty-Three (33/6)

The 33 is the most influ-ential of all numbers. It is the Master of Healing Love. The 33 combines the 11 and the 22 and brings their potential to another level. When expressed to the fullest, the 33 lacks all personal ambition and instead focuses its consi-derable abilities toward the spiritual uplifting of mankind. What makes the 33 especially impressive, is the high level of sincere devotion. This is shown in its determination to seek understanding and wisdom before preaching to others. The 33 in full force is extremely rare. The 33 is on the journey of discovering its powerful healing energy through an open heart and unconditional love.

5

THE BIRTHDAYS'

The birthday is a supporting influence added to the Life Path. Think of it as a modifier to the Life Path. These are traits that you brought into this life much as with the more important and dominating traits shown by the Life Path.

5.1. THE NUMBER ONE

The number 1 energy suggests an increased measure of executive ability and leadership qualities than you path may have indicated. A birthday on day 1 of any month gives greater will power and self-confidence, and very often a rather original approach. This 1 energy may diminish your ability and desire to handle details, preferring instead to paint with a broad brush. You may be sensitive, but your feeling stay rather repressed 2.

5.2. THE NUMBER TWO

Your birth on the 2nd day of the month adds a degree of emotion, sensitivity, and intuition to your reading. The 2 is a very social number allowing you to make friends easily and quickly. Yet you are apt to have a rather nervous air in the company of a large group. You have a warmhearted nature and emotional understanding that constantly seeks affection. You are more prone than most to become depressed and moody, as emotions can turn inward and cause anxiety and mental turmoil. It can be hard for you to bounce back to reality when depression sets in.

5.3. THE NUMBER THREE

Being born on the 3rd day of the month is likely to add a good bit of vitality to your life. The energy of 3 allows you bounce back rapidly from setbacks, physical or mental. There is a restlessness in your nature, but you seem to be able to portray an easygoing, sometimes "couldn't care less" attitude. You have a natural ability to express yourself in public, and you always make a very good impression. Good with words, you excel in writing, speaking, and possibly singing. You are energetic and always a good conversationalist. You have a keen imagination, but you tend to scatter your energies and become involved with too may superficial matters. You are affectionate and loving, but sometimes too sensitive. You are subject to rapid ups and downs.

5.4. THE NUMBER FOUR

Being born on the 4th day of the month should help make you a better manager and organiser. You may be more responsible and self-disciplined than your Life Path suggested because of this date. Sincere and honest, you are a serious and hard working individual. Limitations may be imposed by this 4 energy, especially if this number is active elsewhere in your reading. Your feelings are likely to seem somewhat repressed at times. The number 4 has something of an inhibiting effect on your ability to show and express affections, as feeling are very closely regulated and controlled. Even if it by itself, you are apt to be much more practical, rational, and conscious of details. There is a good deal of rigidity and stubbornness associated with the number 4.

5.5. THE NUMBER FIVE

With a birthday on the 5th of the month you are inclined to work well with people and enjoy them. You are talented and versatile, very good at presenting ideas. You may have a tendency to get itchy feet at times and need change and travel. You tend to be very progressive, imaginative and adaptable. Your mind is quick, clever and analytical. A restlessness in your nature may make you a bit impatient and easily bored with routine. You may have a tendency to shirk responsibility.

5.6. THE NUMBER SIX

A birthday on the 6th of the month adds a tone of responsibility, helpfulness, and understanding to your natural inclinations. Those born on the sixth are more apt to be open and honest with everyone, and more caring about family and friends, too. This is a number associated with responsibility and caring.

5.7. THE NUMBER SEVEN

Born on the 7th day of month gives you a tendency to be something of a perfectionist and makes you more individualistic in many ways. Your mind is good at deep mental analysis and complicated reasoning. You are very psychic and sensitive, and you should usually follow your hunches. You may not take orders too well, so you may want to work along or in a situation where you can be the boss. This birthday gives a tendency to be somewhat self-centered and a little stubborn.

5.8. THE NUMBER EIGHT

Born on the 8th day of the month, you have a special gift for business, as you can conceive and plan on a grand scale. You have good executive skills and you're a good judge of values. You should try to own your own business, because you have such a strong desire to be in control. You are generally reliable when it comes to handling money; you can be trusted in this regard. Idealistic by nature, you are never too busy to spend some time on worthwhile causes, especially if managerial support are needed. There is much potential for material success associated with this number.

5.9. THE NUMBER NINE

Your birth on the 9th day of the month adds a tone of idealism and humanitarianism to your nature. You become one who can work easily with people because you are broadminded, tolerant and generous. You are ever sensitive to others' needs and feelings, and even if the other numbers in your core makeup don't show it, you are very sympathetic and compassionate. Your feeling run deep and you often find yourself in dramatically charged situations. This 9 energy always tends to give more that it gets.

5.10. THE NUMBER TEN

Your birth on the 10th day of the month adds a tone of independence and extra energy to your Life Path. The number 1 energy suggest more executive ability and leadership qualities than you path may have indicated. A birthday on the 10th of any month gives greater will power and self-confidence, and very often a rather original approach. This 1 energy may diminish your ability and desire to handle details, preferring instead to paint with a broad brush. You are sensitive, but your feeling stay somewhat repressed. You have a compelling manner that can be dominating in many situations.

5.11. THE NUMBER ELEVEN

Your birth on the 11th day of the month makes you something of a dreamer and an idealist. You work well with people because you know how to use persuasion rather than force. There is a strong spiritual side to your nature, and you may have intuitive qualities inherent in your make up, too. You are very aware and sensitive, though often temperamental. Although you have a good mind and you are very analytical, you may not be comfortable in the business world. You are definitely creative and this influence tends to make you more of a dreamer than a doer.

5.12. THE NUMBER TWELVE

Being born on the 12th day of the month (3 energy) is likely to add a good bit of vitality to your life. The energy of 3 allows you bounce back rapidly from setbacks, physical or mental. There is a restlessness in your nature, but you seem to be able to portray an easygoing, sometimes "couldn't care less" attitude. You have a natural ability to express yourself in public, and you always make a very good impression. Good with words, you excel in writing, speaking, and possibly singing. You are energetic and always a good conversationalist. You have a keen imagination, but you tend to scatter your energies and become involved with too may superficial matters. Your mind is practical and rational despite this tendency to jump about. You are affectionate and loving, but very sensitive. You are subject to rapid ups and downs.

5.13. THE NUMBER THIRTEEN

Being born on the 13th day of the month should help make you a better manager and organiser, but it may also give you a tendency to dominate people a bit. You may be more responsible and self-disciplined than your Life Path suggested because of this date. Sincere and honest, you are a serious, hard working individual. Limitations may be imposed by this 4 energy, especially if there is additional indications the number elsewhere in your number. Your feeling are likely to seem somewhat repressed at times. Even if it by itself, you are apt to be much more practical, rational, and conscious of details. Your intolerance and insistence on complete accuracy can be irritating to some.

5.14. THE NUMBER FOURTEEN

With a birthday on the 14th of the month (5 energy) you are inclined to work well with people and enjoy them. You are talented and versatile, very good at presenting ideas, and you are also very good at organisation and systematising. You may have a tendency to get itchy feet at times and need change and travel. You tend to be very progressive, imaginative and adaptable. Your mind is quick, clever and analytical. A restlessness in your nature may make you a bit impatient and easily bored with routine, and rebel against it. You have a tendency to shirk responsibility.

5.15. THE NUMBER FIFTEEN

With a birthday on the 15th of any month, you are apt to have really strong attachments to home, family and domestic scene. The 1 and 5 equaling 6, provide the sort of energy that makes you an excellent parent or teacher. You are very responsible and capable. This is an attractive and an attracting influence. You like harmony in your environment and strive to maintain it. You tend to learn by observation rather than study and research. You may like to cook, but you probably don't follow recipes. This number shows artistic leanings and would certainly support an talents that may be otherwise in your makeup. You're a very generous and giving person, but perhaps a bit stubborn in ways.

5.16. THE NUMBER SIXTEEN

Your birth on the 16th day of the month gives a sense of loneliness and generally the desire to work alone. You are relatively inflexible, and insist on your being independent. You need a good deal of time to rest and to meditate. You are introspective and a little stubborn. Because of this, it may not be easy for you to maintain permanent relationships, but you probably will as you are very much into home and family. This birth day inclines to interests in the technical, the scientific, and to the religious or the unknown realm of spiritual explorations. The date gives you a tendency to seek unusual approaches and makes your style seem a little different and unique to those around you. Your intuition is aided by the day of your birth, but most of your actions are bedded in logic, responsibility, and the rational approach. You may be emotional, but have a hard time expressing these emotions. Because of this, there may be some difficulty in giving or receiving affection.

5.17. THE NUMBER SEVENTEEN

Your birth on the 17th day of the month suggests that you are very fortune financially, because this date is very good for business interest and a solid business sense. Although you are probably very honest and ethical, this birthday enables you to be shrewd and successful in the world of business and commercial enterprise. You have excellent organisational, managerial, and administrative capabilities enabling you to handle large projects and significant amounts of money with relative ease. You are ambitious and highly goal-oriented, although you may be better at starting projects than you are at finishing them. A sensitivity in your nature, often repressed below the surface of awareness, makes it hard to give or receive affection.

5.18. THE NUMBER EIGHTEEN

Your birthday on the 18th day of the month suggests than you are one who can work well with a group, but still remain someone who needs to maintain individual identity. There is a humanistic or philanthropic approach to business circumstances in which you find yourself. You may have good executive abilities, as you are very much the organiser and administrator. You are broad-minded, tolerant and generous; a compassionate person that can inspire others with imaginative ideas. Some of your feelings may be expressed, but even more of them are apt to be repressed. There is a lot of drama in your personality and in the way you express yourself to others. Oddly enough, you don't expect as much in return as you give.

5.19. THE NUMBER NINETEEN

Your birth on the 19th day of the month adds a tone of independence and extra energy to your Life Path, but poses a number of obstacles to overcome before you are able to be as independent as you would like. The number 1 energy suggests more executive ability and leadership qualities than your path may have indicated. A birthday on the 19th of any month gives greater will power and self-confidence, and very often a rather original approach;

but with this, a somewhat self-centered approach to life that may be in conflict with some of the other influences in your life. This 1 energy may diminish your ability and desire to handle details, preferring instead to paint with a broad brush. You are sensitive, but your feeling stay somewhat repressed. You have a compelling manner that can be dominating in many situations. You do not tend to follow convention or take advice very well. Consequently, you tend to learn through experience; sometimes hard experiences. The 19/1 is a loner number and you may experience feelings of being alone even if you are married. You may take on a tendency to be nervous and anger more easily than your Life Path number suggests.

5.20. THE NUMBER TWENTY

Your birth on the 20th day of the month adds a degree of emotion, sensitivity, and intuition to your reading. The 2 energy provided here is very social, allowing you to make friends easily and quickly. Yet you are apt to have a rather nervous air in the company of a large group. You have a warmhearted nature and emotional understanding that constantly seeks affection. You are very prone to become depressed and moody, as emotions can turn inward and cause anxiety and mental turmoil. It can be hard for you to bounce back to reality when depression sets in. When things are going well, you can go just as far the other way and become extremely affectionate.

5.21. THE NUMBER TWENTY-ONE

Being born on the 21st day of the month (3 energy) is likely to add a good bit of vitality to your life. The energy of 3 allows you bounce back rapidly from setbacks, physical or mental. There is a restlessness in your nature, but you seem to be able to portray an easygoing, sometimes "couldn't care less" attitude. You have a natural ability to express yourself in public, and you always make a very good impression. Good with words, you excel in writing, speaking, and possibly singing. You are energetic and always a good conversationalist. You have a keen imagination, but you tend to scatter your energies and become involved with too may superficial matters. Your mind is practical and rational despite this tendency to jump about. You are affectionate and loving, but very sensitive. You are subject to rapid ups and downs.

5.22. THE NUMBER TWENTY-TWO

While sometimes employing unorthodox approaches, you are capable of handling large scale undertakings, assuming great responsibility, and working long and hard towards their completion. Often, especially in the early part of life, there is rigidity or stubbornness, and a tendency to repress feelings. Idealistic, you work for the greater good with a good deal of inner strength and charisma. An extremely capable organiser, but likely to paint with broad strokes rather than detail. You are very aware and intuitive. You are subject to a good deal of nervous tension.

5.23. THE NUMBER TWENTY-THREE

With a birthday on the 23rd of the month (5 energy) you are inclined to work well with people and enjoy them. You are talented and versatile, very good at presenting ideas. You may have a tendency to get itchy feet at times and need change and travel. You tend to be very progressive, imaginative and adaptable. Your mind is quick, clever and analytical. A restlessness in your nature may make you a bit impatient and easily bored with routine. You may have a tendency to shirk responsibility.

Very sociable, you make friends easily and you are an excellent traveling companion.

5.24. THE NUMBER TWENTY-FOUR

Born on the 24th, you have a greater capacity for responsibility and helping others than may have shown in your life path. You may also become the mediator and peacemaker in inharmonious situations. Devoted to family, you tend to manage and protect. This birth date adds to the emotional nature and perhaps to the sensitivities. Affections are important to you; both the giving and the receiving.

5.25. THE NUMBER TWENTY-FIVE

Your birth on the 25th day of the month (7 energy) modifies your life path by giving you some special interest in technical, scientific, or other complex and often hard to understand subjects. You may become something of a perfectionist and a stickler for details. Your thinking is logical and intuitive, rational and responsible. Your feelings may run deep, but you are not very likely to let them show. This birthday makes you a more private person, more introspective and perhaps more inflexible. In friendships you are very cautious and reserved. You are probably inventive, and given to unique approaches and solutions.

5.26. THE NUMBER TWENTY-SIX

Your birth on the 26th day of the month (8 energy) modifies your life path by increasing your capability to function and succeed in the business world. In this environment you have the skills to work very well with others thanks to the 2 and 6 energies combining in this date. There is a marked increase in organisational, managerial, and administrative abilities. You are efficient and handle money very well. Ambitious and energetic, while generally remaining cooperative and adaptable. You are conscientious and not afraid of responsibility. Generally sociable and diplomatic, you tend to use persuasion rather than force. You have a wonderful combination of being good at both the broad strokes and the fine detail; good at starting and continuing. This birthday is practical and realistic, often seeking material satisfaction.

5.27. THE NUMBER TWENTY-SEVEN

Your birth on the 27th day of the month (9 energy) adds a tone of selflessness and humanitarianism to your life path. Certainly, you are one who can work very well with people, but at the same time you need a good bit of time to be by your self to rest and meditate. Regardless of your life path number, there is a very humanistic and philanthropic approach in most of things that you do. This birthday helps you be broadminded, tolerant, generous and very cooperative. You are the type of person who uses persuasion rather than force to achieve your ends. You tend to be very sensitive to others' needs and feelings, and you able to give much in the way of friendship without expecting a lot in return.

5.28. THE NUMBER TWENTY-EIGHT

Your birth on the 28th day of the month (1 energy) adds a tone of independence and extra energy to your Life Path. The number 1 energy suggest more executive ability and leadership qualities than you path may have indicated. A birthday on the 28th of any month gives greater will power and self-confidence, and very often a rather original approach. Unlike much of the other 1 energy, this birthday is one that endow with the ability to start a job and continue on until it is finished. You may prefer to use the broad brush, but you can handle details as well. You are sensitive, but your feeling stay somewhat repressed. You have a compelling manner that can be dominating in many situations.

5.29. THE NUMBER TWENTY-NINE

Your birthday on the 29th adds a tone of idealism to your nature. You are imaginative and creative, but rather uncomfortable in the business world. You are very aware and sensitive, with outstanding intuitive skills and analytical abilities. The 29 reduces to 11, one of the master numbers which often produces much nervous tension. This is the birthday of the dreamer rather than the doer. You do, however, work very well with people.

5.30. THE NUMBER THIRTY

Your birthday on the 30th day of the month shows individual self-expression is necessary for your happiness. You tend to have a good way of expressing yourself with words, certainly in a manner that is clear and understandable. You have a good chance of success in fields requiring skill with words. You can be very dramatic in your presentation and you may be a good actor or a natural mimic. You have a vivid imagination that can assist you in becoming a good writer or story-teller. Strong in your opinions, you always tend to think you are on the right side of an issue. There may be a tendency to scatter your energies and have a lot of loose ends in your work. You may have significant artistic talent and be very creative.

5.31. THE NUMBER THIRTY-ONE

Your birthday suggests that you are a good organiser and

manager, an energetic and dependable worker; attributes often showing success in the business world. Serious and sincere, you have the patience and determination necessary to accomplish a great deal. Your approach can be original, but often rigid and stubborn. Sensitivity may be present, but feeling are likely to be repressed. You are good with detail and insist on accuracy, but at times scatter energies. Practical thinker, but not without imagination. You love travel and don't like to live alone. You should probably marry early, for responsibility is necessary for your stability.

6

THE ESSENCE

An additional cycle used in numerology is associated with the name rather than the birth date. This timing method uses the letters in the name in what might be called transits of the name, to arrive at this important cycle information that is called the Essences. The transit begins at birth with the first letter of your first name, the first letter of your middle name, and the first letter of your last name, their values totaled, defining the tone of the year from birth to age one. Then we will go on with these transits finding the Essence of each year of the life.

You'll need to recall those letter values, so here is chart for easy reference:

1	2	3	4	5	6	7	8	9
A	B	C	D	E	F	G	H	I
J	K	L	M	N	O	P	Q	R
S	T	U	V	W	X	Y	Z	

Begin with the first letter of your first name. Each letter in this name will last a number of years (from 1 to 9) depending on its numerology number designation. Thus, if the first name was David, a D would be placed under the F (for First Name) column on each of the first 4 years or rows. The value of D is 4. The next year (row) would get a single A, then V for 4 years, I for the next 9, and finally, the last D for the next 4. This would fill the F column for the first 21 years. Then, you would start over and repeat the process using this first name. If you were going to progress the chart through age 60, a third set of the letter in David would be used which would actually progress the chart (under the letter F) to age 63.

Next, you would follow this procedure under the M for middle name. In the chart the name Michael would have the first 4 years filled with the letter M, the 9 years of I, 3 of C, 8 of H, 1 A, 5 Es, and 3 Ls. Since there are 33 years filled with this name, only two sets would be used to progress the middle name past age 60.

Finally, the last name would be set in using the same process.

After the name has been set on the chart in this fashion, the next task is to fill in the 'Letter Value' column. For the name David Michael McClain, the first year would show D M M each having a value of 4. So 4 would be placed under F, M, and L. This process would be followed for each year.

6.1. ESSENCE OF TRANSIT

Under the column entitled 'essence of transit', total the letter value (for the first, middle and last name letters) for each year, and show the single digit or master number which is derived from this total. This is the Essence for the year (birthday to birthday).

Here are readings for each Essence:

1 2 3 4 5 6 7 8 9

6.1.1. Essence One

The Essence of the number 1 signals a time when you are

developing new ideas and enlarging on projects that have been around for a while. This will be a period that will bring the opportunity for marked increase in your personal status and recognition. This Essence is often an opportunity to turn a life-long avocation into a money-making vocation. Many new friends and business associations are likely no now. Your status in the world may grow now, and you may get some recognition for your achievements. One thing may lead to another and you may find many alterations in your life during this essence.

If this essence remains in effect for 3 years or more. Because this Essence is in effect for such a long period of time, its meaning with regard to change is somewhat confusing. In some cases, this foretells of a series of dramatic ongoing changes, or one considerable change with many years between the beginning and the finale of the alteration.

The effects of this Essence in a number 1 Personal Year are greatly amplified. It will be very hard for you to choose between the opportunities during this period. You are apt to run into some frustrating situations. You need to be prepared to make careful choices now with an eye on the future value of decisions as opposed to what feels good at the moment.

6.1.2. Essence Two

The Essence of the number 2 is a cycle when everything seems to be consolidating and this is decidedly a period of growth. But often the growth is not without reversals, and there is much emphasis on cooperation and patience. You may find yourself developing relationships, or trying very hard to develop a good relationship. You will likely find yourself working with and hopefully helping others.

Conversely, you can expect to get much help from others now. This is apt to be a period of slow development, delays, roadblocks, and obstacles, and the period can be one of great frustration for you in certain ways. There can be a lot of emotions associated with the 2 Essence, and you may become much more sensitive now. Lowered energy and vitality may be experienced throughout the cycle. Confrontations are difficult now, but often necessary.

The 2 Essence remaining in your lifepath for a lengthy period may produce nervous tension due to prolonged high emotions and/or deep frustration due to the delays and problems encountered.

When this Essence is in effect during a number 2 personal year, emotional conflicts may heighten the tension, upset the sensitivity, and even affect the health. Self-control and a disciplined approach can help maintain a harmonious balance. Plan to move forward slowly, despite periodic detours.

6.1.3. Essence Three

The Essence of the number 3 is a very special time when you feel and experience the joy of living to its utmost. This is a very enjoyable time in your life. You are apt to be making a lot of new friends and renewing old friendships. This is a time for love affairs and expanding the social circle; many activities and good times. You are likely to travel a good bit during this Essence.

The other factor that is associated with the Essence of 3 is that of expression. This is a very good time for you to be interested in the development of creative work, particularly works that involve words...singing, acting, writing. This should be a busy time advancing your talents with classes or study, or for starting or expanding business ventures involving creative endeavors.

Optimism is the operative word for this cycle. This is a very pleasant period, but you must beware of a tendency now to scatter your energies.

This long period may allow a significant creative development in a positive and happy time of your life.

6.1.3.1. Essence Three with Personal year Three

Since you are enjoying this three Essence along with a 3 personal year, you may have a great deal of difficulty maintaining your sense of self-discipline. Having too much fun can be a long term mistake. Likewise, this is probably to be a very restless time for you as you may be on the go a great deal.

6.1.4. Essence Four

During this number 4 Essence the events and opportunities coming your way will emphasise a more serious tone. This is a time to buckle down and put the affairs of your life in order. Your attention is apt to be drawn to more practical interests such as dealing with financial matters and your work. The development of opportunities in your life now requires a practical and realistic view along with a lot of hard work, effort, determination and discipline. In many ways you are apt to feel a sense of restriction in your life for a while and you may face some setbacks as the pace of progress slows somewhat. This is a building time and the building is sometimes painfully slow.

Since the 4 essence is with you for several years, this period is apt to feel like a never ending struggle. Yet significant gains or accomplishments may be the reward for your hard work and determination during this essence.

Since this Essence accompanies a personal year number 4, the feelings of being in a rut are not uncommon. The repressive conditions may be in your mind more than in the work at hand, but the feeling will be there just the same. Be objective about the obstacles you really face because it may be that they are not as formidablc as you think.

6.1.5. Essence Five

With the Essence of the number 5 you will find that the events and opportunities coming your way will emphasise freedom and change. Your experiences during this cycle will be sudden, unusual, and unexpected, and you are apt to be dealing with constantly changing circumstances and activities. The ventures in your life now will stress progress, new ideas, and probably new friends. Travel is very likely. There should be a caution here to avoid tendencies to go off in every direction and scatter your forces. Choose your opportunities carefully and thoughtfully. Freedom is great, but be sure to use it in constructive ways that help others and yourself.

A long period of 5 Essence suggests that it is apt to be a very free-wheeling period. Unless some self-discipline is exercised, most of the energy is likely to be scattered with little accomplishment. If this scattering occurs, there may be feelings of deep frustration.

This may be a period when you are too free-wheeling and unrestrained. Constant change is not always constant growth and development. Try to maintain a balanced and thoughtful approach to problems and opportunities. Control self-centered interests.

6.1.6. Essence Six

The 6 Essence focuses circumstances and opportunities on

the home, the family, and largely on domestic matters. This time is associated with responsibility, but usually the job is close to home or involving those nearest to you, including your close friends. If you are single, this Essence is a very good time for marriage; if married, this is a good time for your marriage. It is a good time to surface any problems that may exist in the marriage and deal with them before they become more serious.

This is also a time for children, and it may be a time to have a child. The 6 essence also may and often does involve you in service to your community in some way; assuming responsibility for those outside your immediate family. This is more common if you are older and the need for your services in the immediate family is not apparent.

The idea of intense responsibility is very much a part of your life during this period. Ideally, you will accept responsibilities and thrive in its execution. Resistance to duty now may impart a sense of suppression or isolation. On the other hand, if you meet challenges now, you are apt to become handsomely repaid with love and the devotion of those close to you.

Responsibilities may never seem greater, but the rewards for accepting obligations and meeting the test may never be greater either. This is a year when feeling emotions and sharing them with someone close to you can help the family or community grow stronger and more cohesive. This may be a time when the size of your family grows larger.

6.1.7. Essence Seven

During the essence of the number 7, many of the events in your life now will often involve study, a sense of isolation, and an inwardly focused attitude toward yourself. A time of looking for an understanding of fundamentals and pursuing new interests has arrived. You are likely to find yourself withdrawing for a time of reflection and perhaps even meditation, hopefully comfortable with a chance for repose.

Since the 7 essence is to be with you for a while, look forward to a time of internality and spiritual growth. You may grow away from others and become much more introspective.

This can be a period when you become very moody and withdrawn. You may have to force yourself to be social because this seems like an aspect of life that is not important now. While you may actually enjoy your solitude, guard against signs of depression.

6.1.8. Essence Eight

The number 8 essence suggests that the trend of events will be pointed toward getting ahead in a material sense and basically taking care of business. This essence normally marks a period when the business and professional reputation is enhanced and ripens. You are apt to reap financial gain now, building or expanding current ventures. Common sense and good judgments will help you achieve goals and make some real progress. This is apt to be a period when you work very hard.

This long period 8 essence may be an indication that you are very focused on issues of the career, power, and status. You may have to be reminded to stop occasionally to "smell the roses."

6.1.8.1. Essence eight with personal year eight

When the 8 essence is joined by an 8 personal year, the stress of you devotion to "getting ahead" can be great. While this is an important period for you relative to the career, your power and status, it is also a time that can take a toll on other aspects of your life.

6.1.9. Essence Nine

With the Essence of the number 9 life will tend to have a very dramatic or emotional flair. Your feelings and reactions to events will be very acute. Often this Essence denotes the ending to a significant endeavor, and a marked change in interests of some kind. Usually, additional freedom is a byproduct of the concluding affair. If you are single, there is likely to be an intense or emotional romance. Frequently, this Essence shows involvement with humanitarian endeavors are a constant during the essence period. Endings now may lead to a more useful life.

The fact that this is such a long period of 9 essence suggests that it is apt to be a very extended period of passionate feelings, a long drawn out love affair with a prolonged ending, or perhaps a sustained effort of some sort. This may be an emotionally draining year which completions coming only with great difficulty. Clear thinking will be difficult but it is a must.

For the Essences of the number 11 and 22, refer to 2 and 4 respectively. However, the 11 Essence has a very strong spiritual overtone about it, while the 22 Essence may signal a time of significant achievement or venture.

7

CHALLENGES

In numerology, the roadblocks faced in life are called challenges. Challenges are weak points in our Life Path. They are weak links in the chain of life which must be overcome for us to grow and develop properly. We learn by meeting the challenges and mastering them. The nature of challenges are shown in the Life Path.

7.1. CALCULATING CHALLENGES

The rule for calculating challenges is just the opposite of pinnacles. Each challenge is represent by a number and the number reflects the tone of the confrontation of the period. The challenge number is written in the birth date. We will again use the month, the day and the year of birth in this calculation. The first step will be to reduce each of these components to a single digit base number. Thus, December 14, 1968, would become month 3 (1+2), day 5 (1+4), and year 6 (1+9+6+8=24; 2+4=6).

The first challenge is derived by finding the difference between the month and day of birth. In our example, this would be 5-3=2 first challenge.

The second challenge is identified by finding the difference between the day of birth with the year of birth. The example would be 6-5=1; the number 1 for a second challenge.

The third challenge is identified by finding the difference between the first and second challenge. Our example would have an 2-1=1 third challenge.

The fourth challenge is identified by finding the difference between the month and the year. Our example would produce a 6-3=3 fourth challenge.

The timing of challenges varies for each of the first nine Life Path numbers, and is the same as the pinnacles. The timing for the master number 11 is the same a Life Path 2, and the master number 22 is same as the Life Path 4. The first challenge begins at birth. This challenge ending is calculated by subtracting the Life Path number from 36. In our December 14, 1968 example (a 5 Life Path), the end of first challenge is at age 31. The second challenge will be in effect for 9 year or until age 40. The third challenge will also be in effect for 9 years ending at age 49. The 4th challenge beginning at age 50 will be in effect for the remaining years of life. You may get more help on calculating the challenges on worksheet form.

If you correctly reduced the month, day and year to a single digit (no master number), the difference between the two numbers must be from 0 to 8. Here are reading of each of the challenges:

The Challenge of the Number:

0 1 2 3 4 5 6 7 8

7.1.1. Challenge Zero

The obstacles life during this period may not be many, or they may be coming from all directions. The challenge of the number 0 is called the challenge of choice. You are likely to have difficulty acting on your preferences. You are perfectly capable of analysing a situation and realistically comparing possible solutions. The challenge of 0 may make bring this decision to requisite action very difficult for you. To overcome the challenge, it should be understood that you must have the faith in your own abilities to the extent that you can analyse, make a choice, then act with ease and comfort.

This challenge is one that is normally found on in a highly evolved individual and an individual who can be expected to make your own decisions about life and know where the pitfalls lie. To meet the challenge of 0 you must have control of all of the numbers; the independence of 1, the diplomacy of 2, the optimism of 3, the application of 4, the understanding of 5, the adjustment of 6, the wisdom of the 7, the constructive power of 8, the universal service of 9. In other words, to meet the challenge of 0 in your life, you must be a very gifted person.

7.1.2. Challenge One

The challenge of the number 1 suggests that in these years, you are likely to feel dominated by others with strong influence, probably parents or others with whom you compete. The challenge of the number 1 is avoidance of being dominated, but doing so in a fashion that does not impose upon or dominate others. With the challenge of the number 1 it's extremely important to control the ego, and avoid the negative aspect of individuality. False pride, pomposity, egotism are issues to be guarded against now. You are now in a period of learning about self-reliance and how to solve your own problems independently. Learn to rely on your wit and your intelligence, avoiding argumentation and resentfulness.

7.1.3. Challenge Two

The challenge of the number 2 suggests you are likely to be extremely sensitive and more or less brimming with feeling. You find it hard to work with people because your are afraid of being criticised or, worse yet, ignored. You have a good deal of self-doubt and a definite lack of self confidence. There is a tendency to constantly worry about the opinion that others have of you. There is likewise a tendency to use this sensitivity in a negative way. Used more positively, your keen sensitivities can be a significant strength, allowing you to be acutely aware of so much of with others rarely perceive. But during this period it will be hard for you to assert yourself and make decisions.

You will shy away from positions of authority and responsibility. This can be a time for accumulation of wisdom, as you show patience and pay close attention to detail. Try not to take things too personally. Friendships are a source of deep satisfaction to you during this time. Respect your ability to compromise and grow in a quiet way. Do not let details overwhelm you and keep you from seeing the big picture. Plan for slow growth rather than immediate gain.

7.1.4. Challenge Three

The challenge of the number 3 suggests a tendency to scatter talents and try to do too many things at once during this period of your life. You may have a fine imagination and a gift for words, but you find it hard to express yourself effectively. Though you know you should cultivate friends and be sociable, you tend to be somewhat reclusive and defensive. You may have a talent for writing, acting, or speaking, but you are reluctant to involve yourself with these sorts of activities because you do not like to face the prospects of criticism. You are expressing yourself with a negative emphasis, hiding your creative talents behind a wall of shyness. You must strive to develop yourself in a social and in a creative sense.

7.1.5. Challenge Four

The challenge of the number 4 suggests a difficulty with work. Either you simply don't like to work, don't like the work your are forced to do, or you have difficulty completing tasks and working efficiently. You may be careless and lack a sense of practicality. Often this challenge makes it hard to see the forest for the trees when it comes to work and obligations. It is important for you to learn patience, understanding and the practical, common sense way of dealing with mundane responsibilities. You may also need to learn the importance of working within the parameters of a time schedule.

7.1.6. Challenge Five

The challenge of the number 5 suggests that your challenge is to overcome the desire and the demand for freedom at any price. This challenge number is very difficult to handle because, with it, you are apt to be extremely impulsive; you want to try everything at least once, and you are rather unstable in many ways. Change may be necessary for you, but it must be handled in an intelligent and controlled manner. Make certain that the desire for change is not associated with a desire to escape responsibility. In any event, this challenge requires that you learn as early as possible in life to control your impulses.

7.1.7. Challenge Six

The challenge of the number 6 suggests that you may have difficulties because of your insistence on extremely high standards. You are apt to appear authoritarian, intolerant, and a little self-righteous. It is hard for others to live up to your standards of expectation. Many of your considerable talents for balancing situations are used with a negative emphasis. Avoid creating friction in relationships and strive for harmony. You must learn that your diplomatic approach will only be appreciated if others feel that their needs are met, their desires understood, their point of view respected. You must learn to allow others to set their own pace, make their own rules. This challenge requires learning unconditional love and acceptance.

7.1.8. Challenge Seven

The challenge of the number 7 suggests difficulties brought on by your discomfort with your own inner feelings; feelings of a reserved attitude and unexpressed emotions. You may feel unable to better your situation, or to change and improve circumstances. There is a tendency with this challenge to be a chronic critic and complainer, while offering little or nothing as a suggest to correct the faults that are found. The sense of discrimination is strong, but it is expressed in a very negative way. A sense of false pride tends to keep your real feelings buried beneath the surface. Avoid a tendency to approach people in a very reserved and aloof way, and develop faith in your own abilities rather than dwelling on your limitations. Marriage is apt to be delayed until this challenge is overcome, or if married, this can be a difficult time.

7.1.9. Challenge Eight

The challenge of the number 8 suggests an early life assumption that satisfaction can only be gained and safeguarded by adequate material accumulation. There's likely to be considerable effort exerted to attain money, status, and power, sometimes to the exclusion of almost all else. The number 8 challenge indicates that you are/

were using your concern with material matters with negative emphasis. You must learn to use your ability to gain money, status and power with a sense of proportion and an awareness of the relation of material affairs to other matters, and deal with the material world in a comfortable manner.

8

THE SPECIAL TRAITS AND LESSON

Now we'll look at your name with respect to the numbei of times that the same number repeats, or when certain numbers fail to be represented in your name. The repetition of numbers may show special talents that you possess. The absence of numbers suggests an issue relating to the nature of the number. Some numerologists suggest that the absence of a number reflects a karmic debt carried over from a previous lifetime. The norm in distribution of numbers in the name is somewhat hazy because some names are very short and others are very long. The average name has 15 to 19 letters in it.

If your name is significantly longer or shorter than 15-19 letters, you must make adjustments accordingly. Now, make a count of each of the numbers in your name as given in the following example:

A M I T A B H   B A C H H A N
1 4 9 2 1 2 8   2 1 3 8 8 1 5

As you can see, we have the average number of 4s. We have more than the average 1s and 2s and 8S. We have fewer than average 3s, 5s, 6s, 7s and 9s.

Be aware that if a missing or less than average number is represented in the subject's core numbers (the Life Path, Expression, or Soul Urge), the karmic deficiency is diminished, if not completely eliminated. For example, if an individual did not have the number 5 in his name, but his Life Path number is 5, he would have little difficulty handling the deficiency shown by the absence of the number.

8.1. ONE

Average. With 3 ones in your name, it appears you have sufficient leadership skills, initiative, and ample individuality to get along fine in life.

No 1s or fewer than average. With few or no ones in your name, you may find it hard to stand up for your rights and leadership may be a very difficult trait for you to develop.

More than average 1s. With more than the expected number of ones in your name, you may be very headstrong and even overly assertive in your will to lead. Avoid being too quick to demand your own way.

8.2. TWO

Average. You have a normal and natural desire and ability to associate with others. You are tactful and diplomatic enough to get along fine in the world. Cooperation is no problem for you.

No 2s. You lack patience with people and you may be insensitive sometimes because of this. Cooperation is a trait that must be learned.

Many 2s. You're very considerate of others and have a flair for compromise. Harmony and agreement making may be a major career advantage. You are faithful and adaptable, even to the extent of giving too much. You have a significant appreciate of the arts.

8.3. THREE

Average. If you have a pair of 3s in your name, your imagination and creative talents most likely are in the normal range. You express ideas and feeling with natural ways. Although you may not be described as the life of the party, you know how to have fun and enjoy good company.

No 3s or less than average. This doesn't say that you are dull, but it does suggest that you may have to be stimulated into enjoying yourself. You are not a romantic and one to base decisions of fanciful ideas. Creative ideas may be rare. Of course, if you have a 3 Life Path, Expression, or Soul Urge, this may not be such a problem.

Many 3s. You have more than your fair share of creative talent. You have the kind of imagination that makes you special in music, painting, writing, design, or other artistic endeavors. Indeed, you may tend to scatter yourself a bit at times. You have a "gift for gab," and express yourself well.

8.4. FOUR

Average. If you have at least one 4 in your name, your ability to concentrate and apply yourself to a task will allow you to get along well in the world much of the time. The number 4 gives us common sense and the desire to build or develop things. The number 4 needs order and structure.

No 4s or less than average. If there is no 4 in your name, you will not likely be famous for your common sense and focus on mundane tasks. This trait will be well hidden if you have the number 4 as one of the core numbers, but if this is not the case, you may be a very unstructured and disorganized person. The concept of steady building and developing will be something that you must learn the hard way.

Many 4s. If you have more than the average of one 4 in your name, your ability to engage yourself in concrete plans will be a strong trait. You know the value of things and have the willingness to work toward long range goals. You understand details and respect law and order. You may tend to become too rigid and narrow in your thinking.

8.5. FIVE

Average. If you have the average of four 5s in your name, you enjoy the human trait of having change and variety in your life, at least to a normal degree. You get along well in day-to-day public contact with the world, and adjust to meeting new people, travel, progress, and all of the changes that are part of living.

No 5s or less than average. It is very unusual to have no 5s in a name. If you if you have less than the average number of 5s, you may have a varying degree of difficulty meeting and dealing with people. You will not feel at ease in a crowd, and indeed, you will want to be left alone much of the time. A limitation of 5s makes it hard to face changes. Hopefully, this number will appear in your core so that this absence will merely be viewed as introspection.

Many 5s. With 5 or more 5s, you may have a very restless nature needing much stimulation. It may be hard to apply yourself to any one project because you tend to get too many things going on at the same time. If this number become too heavy in a name, there is a lessening of attention to detail and less respect for law and order. Properly channeled, this excess of 5s aids salesmanship and promotion.

8.6. SIX

Average 6. The average of two 6s produces normal

instincts to protect and cultivate those close to us and even in the larger community. The traits inherent to 6 yield caretakers, teachers, caring parents, and responsible citizens. The number 6 stands for responsibility and nurturing.

No 6 or less than average. With just one 6 or with a name not containing a 6, your sense of duty to those around you is not strong. Indeed, the sense of obligation to fix the world is not strong in many of us. In daily living, the absence of 6s suggests a certain detachment, and problems large and small are handled without becoming very emotional or concerned. Parenting is often too loose and less than demanding.

Many 6s. A more than average number of 6s in the name produces strongly possessed beliefs and emotions. Ideals are strongly held and seldom surrendered. Your humanitarian spirit and sense of generosity may be outstanding traits in your nature. But your leadership and parenting may be too strict and unyielding sometimes. Loyalty is often consider an absolute necessity. Traditions are strong.

8.7. SEVEN

Average 7. The average of one 7 gives the abilities to analyze, investigate, and learn easily. You have a questioning mind which stimulates reading, study, observation and development of the mind. You have the ability to question and discriminate constructively.

No 7s. The qualities of the 7 are missing in many names making the mysteries of life more difficult to understand and grasp. Without a 7 in your name, you may be less cautious, less analytic, and perhaps not the top of the class when it comes to study. You are less apt to be overly skeptical and demanding of those around you.

Many 7s. If you are that rare individual who has many 7s in your name, it may be said that you "dance to a different drummer." Your mind is highly scientific and proof oriented. You take nothing on faith. Many of your ideas will be considered odd and out of step with most of the world around you. Emotions are very controlled.

8.8. EIGHT

Average 8. If you have the average of at least one 8, you are generally businesslike and self-sufficient in your affairs. You have average abilities to lead, direct and control others if you choose to develop these traits. With an 8 in your name, you can weigh and balance. Business, management, supervising people, and managing money are traits shown by the number 8.

No 8s. Without an 8 in your name it will be more difficult to manage and direct even your own personal affairs. Power, wealth, and leadership roles in life may not be your primary goal. Yet you are apt to suffer less stress because of your attitudes about these issues.

Many 8s. With 2 or more 8s you may have an intensity in your nature that drives toward power and control of others. You have a strong drive to accomplish, work, guide and command. Life may hold many tests and be frustrating at times, but the rewards can be high. Be aware of the stress in your life.

8.9. NINE

Average 9. With the average three 9s (or perhaps with only 2) in your name, you have the sense of compassion, goodwill, and tolerance for your fellow man that is necessary to live in our complicated world. The number 9 is associated with mankind and brotherhood. It produces our willingness to accept different races, colors, religions, and beliefs, and life comfortably in our environment. There is a spiritual understanding and acceptance that is normal and healthy.

No 9 or only one 9 in your name. The lack of 9s in the name, though rare, makes it hard to understand and accept others that are different. There is little feeling of universal or spiritual connection.

Many 9s. With many 9s in your name you may be overly sensitive to the world and become an idealist in some aspect of society. You may be generous to a fault. You may take such issues as religion or philosophy to an extreme.

9

FORECASTING THE FUTURE

Both fun and simple to calculate, these numbers are unique to each of us, allowing us to use numerology to help us make the most of our future paths.

9.1. PERSONAL YEAR NUMBERS

One of the ways numerologists foretell the future is through the calculation and analysis of our Personal Year Numbers. They are calculated using the method we use for finding our Life Path Numbers, except we will substitute a future (or present) year in place of our birth year. For instance, if you would like to determine what your personal year is for the year 2002, you would use the following formula:

Your birth month + Your birth day + Current/ Future Calendar Year

Using the birth date (February 26th) as an example.

2 + 26 + 2002

= 2 + (2 + 6) + (2 + 0 + 0 + 2)

= 2 + 8 + 4

= 14

= 5

Therefore, the personal year number for the year 2002 is 14/5.

And since our birthdays are all different our Personal Year Numbers for any given year will be different, too. Each Personal Year Number has a specific meaning or feel to it which allows us to predict certain influences and situations that will arise during a person's life in that particular year.

9.1.1. Personal Year Number One

This will be a busy year where new dreams and projects are begun. Try to focus on you; a new cycle is about to begin.

9.1.2. Personal Year Number Two

This will be a calm, peaceful year spent with a loved one. Spend as much time with others as possible and relax.

9.1.3. Personal Year Number Three

A communicative year in which you express yourself clearly and ideas flow like wine. Have fun and CREATE!

9.1.4. Personal Year Number Four

This will be a very productive year full of hard work and focus. Don't quit before you finish what needs to be done.

9.1.5. Personal Year Number Five

Your life will change in some way. You may begin taking risks or discover a newfound freedom. If you've always wanted to try something or just need a change, this is the year to do it!

9.1.6. Personal Year Number Six

You will be needed on the home front, supporting and loving those closest to you. Don't forget to maintain a sense of balance.

9.1.7. Personal Year Number Seven

This will be a year spent in solitary contemplation and quiet pursuits of your own desires. Take this time to go deep within yourself.

9.1.8. Personal Year Number Eight

This will be a year of great achievement. You will be very busy on the business end of things. You need to focus on achieving all that you desire this year.

9.1.9. Personal Year Number Nine

Typically, this year will begin with lots of commotion and end with quiet. It signifies the completion of a life cycle. Next year, you will begin anew.

9.2. PERSONAL MONTH NUMBERS

Your Personal Year Numbers, you can discover your Personal Month Numbers as well. After you have calculated a Personal Year Number, simply add the number of the month. Your Personal Month Numbers have the same rhythm as your Personal Year Numbers. If you would like to discover what your Personal Month Number holds in store for you, read the descriptions from the previous section (Personal Year Numbers).

9.3. PINNACLE NUMBERS

Another number system used to forecast your future is

through a group of numbers that numerologists refer to as Pinnacle Numbers. Everyone has FOUR Pinnacle Numbers.

The First Pinnacle Number lasts from the moment you are born to 27 - 35 years of age (depending on your Life Path Number).

The Second Pinnacle Number lasts for nine years following your First Pinnacle Period.

The Third Pinnacle Number represents the following nine years.

The Fourth Pinnacle Number begins after the Third Pinnacle Period ends and will last for the remainder of your life.

Your Pinnacle Numbers indicate what you can achieve during these four major time periods within your life by showing you what you should be doing during each period. Before we find our Pinnacle Numbers, let's determine what ages each of our Pinnacle years will fall within.

1. To determine your First Pinnacle Length, subtract your Life Path Number from 36.
2. To determine your Second Pinnacle Length, add the number nine to the answer of step 1.
3. To determine your Third Pinnacle Length, add the number nine to the answer of step 2.
4. Your Fourth Pinnacle has no finite length.

9.3.1. First Pinnacle Number

To calculate your First Pinnacle Number add your birth month and birth day together. Reduce to a single digit.

9.3.2. Second Pinnacle Number

To calculate your Second Pinnacle Number add your

birth day and birth year together. Reduce to a single digit.

9.3.3. Third Pinnacle Number

To calculate your Third Pinnacle Number add your First and Second Pinnacle Numbers together. Reduce to a single digit.

9.3.4. Fourth Pinnacle Number

To calculate your Fourth Pinnacle Number add your birth month to your birth year. Reduce to a single digit.

10

LOVE AND ROMANCE IN NUMEROLOGY

In this chapter we will learn how each number falls in love, stays in love and feels in love. To find our love match or "soul mate" we should look to our Soul's Urge number. It tells our soul's secrets and this is where love is found. But before we discuss our love compatibility, let's take a look at all the lovers.

10.1. LOVER NUMBER ONE

You are highly romantic and a generous lover. Unexpected gifts and your undivided attention are the norm in your love relationships. Be careful that your need for independence doesn't destroy the romance.

10.2. LOVER NUMBER TWO

You are the gentle soul who longs not only for a lover but a best friend too. You want marriage, family, children and true love on a daily basis. You are as devoted as they come.

10.3. LOVER NUMBER THREE

You are a fun, attractive lover who looks for the same

qualities in a romantic partner. You may be in the relationship for a good time and not a long time—the typical serial monogamist. Your partners don't seem to mind; they're having too much fun.

10.4. LOVER NUMBER FOUR

You are not a romantic. You know exactly what you want in your mate and see that you find the most suitable person for the job. You will probably meet your spouse through the personals. This is a great way to weed out the unacceptables.

10.5. LOVER NUMBER FIVE

You are overflowing with sex appeal and sexual heat. You are a sensuous lover .who quickly jumpss into physically intimate relationships, trying everything at least once. You have difficulty committing yourself and may find yourself falling in love over and over and over again. That's just fine with you - variety is the name of your game!

10.6. LOVER NUMBER SIX

You are not into casual affairs or one-night stands. You want an eternally binding commitment that you can depend on. You are a romantic lover who enjoys bubble baths for two, candlelight dinners, and making love in a bed of rose petals.

10.7. LOVER NUMBER SEVEN

Your criteria are often set very high due to your perfectionist tendencies. You have an ideal lover in your mind that no mortal could ever live up to. You find yourself having secret affairs with people you find interesting. But your need for Mr. or Ms perfect may prevent you from enjoying a deeply loving commitment.

10.8. LOVER NUMBER EIGHT

You don't have time for romance. You need a solid, slim, and attractive partner who will aid you in achieving success. You live in comfort, however, and your partner will enjoy your extravagant lifestyle. To you image is everything. You love; you don't romance.

10.9. LOVER NUMBER NINE

Your love knows no bounds. You are the consummate half soul searching for your lost other half. When you find him or her, be sure to give them all the attention he or she needs; you have a tendency to get sidetracked in the troubles of the world. You also have a tendency toward promiscuity, giving great love to every soul who needs it.

10.10. LOVER NUMBER ELEVEN

You are a tender and gentle lover who likes to be in control. You think of love in terms of a heightened spiritual connection where your two souls (yours and your lover's) cease to be separated for wondrous moments in time, joining on a spiritual plane above. You are an intense lover!

10.11. LOVER NUMBER TWENTY-TWO

You want a serious long-term commitment with a person who has the same interests, goals, and dreams. Like the four, you are not overly romantic; you know exactly what you want.

10.11.1. Soul's Urge Number Compatibility

Now that we know what kind of lover you are, how do we discover who your best partners will be? In numerology, there are certain numbers that are compatible with one another. Placed in three groups, the numbers within each group share a natural, easy compatibility with one another. The groups are:

1. 3 - 6 - 9 (The Artsy Numbers)
2. 1 - 5 - 7 (The Smartsy Numbers)
3. 2 - 4 - 8 (The Money Numbers)

So if you have a Soul's Urge of number 2, your best partner or "soul mate" would be another 2, 4 or 8. Although your Soul's Urge number is the most important number in determining relationship compatibility, there are other numbers that indicate compatibility or incompatibility as well. When analysing your love relationship it is also important to take a look at the following numbers in your charts.

10.11.2. Life Path Numbers

If you have a good Soul's Urge match you can study your Life Path Numbers to determine what each of you will be learning this time and the paths your life will take you down. If you both have similar paths to take it can make for a more "cosmically-in-sync" life together.

10.11.3. Expression Numbers

After you analyse your life path numbers, you might want to take a look at your expression numbers. They will indicate if you have similar interests, values, beliefs, etc. This is a good number to learn about personality and character compatibility. Your Soul's Urge, however, is about love and passion. You must choose which you consider more important in a love relationship.

10.11.4. Maturity Numbers

The last numbers to look at in terms of romantic relationships are your maturity numbers. They indicate the compatibility of your later years. As an interesting side note, if the maturity number is the only compatible number that you share, it might indicate a late marriage. You might even be over 50 years old before you marry.

10.11.5. Counting your Differences

After you have discovered where your love compatibility is strongest with your lover or romantic partner, you may find yourself wondering where your differences or troubles will be. This is where you need to count your differences-or rather, subtract your differences.

Typically, only calculated with your Soul's Urge Number (but you can do it with all of your major five numbers), the calculation to discover your differences is quite simple. You take both of your Soul's Urge Numbers and subtract the smallest number from the largest one. This will be the vibration or energy force that may cause problems within your relationship.

For example, let's say your Soul's Urge Number is 6 and your partner's is 1. The difference will be (6 - 1 = 5). You will need to change or adapt in some way, allowing you and your partner more freedom.

10.11.5.1. Difference of one

You may have issues over control and independence. You will need to respect one another's individuality if your relationship is to succeed.

10.11.5.2. Difference of two

Teamwork is the key to this relationship. You will need to learn to work together and support one another if you want your relationship to work.

10.11.5.3. Difference of three

Talk, talk, and talk some more. You need to understand one another completely; lies and secrets could destroy this relationship.

10.11.5.4. Difference of four

You will struggle with rigidity and structure. You need to learn to practise patience and kindness. Love shouldn't have to be so hard.

10.11.5.5. Difference of five

You will need to change or adapt in some way, allowing you and your partner more freedom.

10.11.5.6. Difference of six

You will need to bring balance to your relationship, learning to become responsible and accepting love as it really is-it's time to let go of the fantasy.

10.11.5.7. Difference of seven

You need to understand and honour aloneness. Too much togetherness may stifle this relationship, creating a superficial and forced atmosphere.

10.11.5.8.. Difference of eight

This relationship is the battle of the "bosses!" You both

want to be in charge and may lose each other in your constant power struggles. You need to support one another and form a loving marriage partnership that has two acting presidents.

11

YOUR INNER DREAMS

The sum of the consonants in your name relates a secret dream, your inner desires, or maybe even fantasies. As a modifier, this aspect of your chart may be considered less important than many of the others because often these remote and deep-seated dreams are never realized. Sometimes, however, when this number has a relationship to another core number, the dream can come true. Strangely, this number is also associated with your personality or how people see you on first meetings. This number may be so strong in your subconscious that you even project the trait as a personality mask.

Here's a chart showing the value of the consonants:

1	2	3	4	5	6	7	8	9
—	B	C	D	—	F	G	H	—
J	K	L	M	N	—	P	Q	R
S	T	—	V	W*	X	Y*	Z	—

* Don't count W or Y as a consonant if it is been used as a vowel in the name.

If the consonants in your name add up to:

1. You dream of being a leader and one who is in charge. You want to be know for your courage,

daring, and original ideas. You seek unconquered heights. People may get a first impression that you are very aggressive and sure of yourself.

2. You dream of close and meaningful relationships, cooperation with those around you; family and friends. You want to be a peacemaker and mediator. You present an image that you are a very pliable and easygoing person who would be very easy to get along with.
3. You dream of artistic expression; writing, painting, music. You would seek to more freely express your inner feeling and obtain more enjoyment from life. You also dream of being more popular, likable, and appreciated.
4. You dream of being a very solid citizen that people can depend upon. You strive for organization and predictable order. You want to be recognized as a person with a plan and the discipline to make that plan work like clockwork.
5. You dream of being totally free and unrestrained by responsibility. You see yourself conversing fluently tongues, mingling with the native in many nations, living for adventure and life experiences. You imagine what you might accomplished if you had the opportunity.
6. You dream of guiding and fostering the perfect family in the perfect home. You crave the devotion from offspring and a loving spouse. You picture yourself in the center of a successful domestic unit.
7. You dream of having the opportunity to read, study, and shut yourself off from worldly distractions. You can see yourself as a teacher, mystic, or ecclesiastic, spending your life in the pursuit of knowledge and learning.

8. You dream of success in the business or political world, of power and control of large material endeavors. You crave authority and recognition of executive skills. Your secret self may have very strong desire to become an entrepreneur.
9. You dream of being creative, intellectual, and universal; the selfless humanitarian. You understand the needy and what to help them. You would love to be a person people count on for support and advice.
11. You dream of casting the light of illumination; of being the true idealist. You secretly believe there is more to life than we can know or prove, and you would like to be provider of the "word" from on high.
12. You dream of being a master organizer and a builder of monumental projects; of guiding a truly huge endeavor. Your secret fantasy is to think big and imagine what could be done for the world. You may also dream of the huge rewards.

12

MODERN NUMEROLOGY

Modern numerologists beleives that there is no scientific or mathematical evidence to show that numbers exhibit these properties. Numbers one to nine are used in present-day numerology to determine character analysis and predict upcoming trends. Other numbers are thought to carry vibrational influences which must also be taken into consideration, as must also the connection of astrology, numbers, and locational addresses.

12.1. ONE

One is the first number used when counting and therefore it is considered to have great power; without it there would be no numbering system as we know it. Every numerical system we are aware of has had one as its initial starting point. As one is common to all numbers, it is often seen as the origin of all things and represents perfection, absolute, and deity in monotheistic faiths. One can be happy, loving, romantic, dynamic and charismatic, but on the downside it can be egotistical, selfish and melodramatic.

12.2. TWO

Two can have many different meanings, representing partnerships and interaction with others on one hand,

and disunion and polarities on the other. In symbolising partnership, two implies that individual achievements are not realistic because accomplishments are best realised through co-operation and teamwork. While duality is required for the formation of life in sexually reproducing species, it is also seen negatively when contrasted with the perfect, unified number one. Two represents polarities such as good and evil, black and white, male and female, left and right.

One pole cannot exist without the other; this idea of complementary relationships is best symbolised with the Yin-Yang symbol. Polarity, though, can also create strife and discord. Two may be considered feminine, intuitive, and corresponds with our protective instincts. Negatively, two can be grasping, overprotective and cranky. The cranky aspect of the number two is derived from the disappointment and dissatisfaction of the human spirit when denied first place in anything.

12.3. THREE

Three solves the discord created in the polarity of two, resulting in a new integration and wholeness. This can be seen in the divisions of a human: mind, body, and spirit makes us whole. Three can also relate to expansiveness and learning through life experiences. It is considered to be lucky, and is often associated with money and good fortune. Three can depict several people joining together to achieve a common goal, whether through a social or professional affiliation. Three also represents communication of all kinds, expression, drama, acting, and humor.

Although three possesses attributes of wisdom, understanding and knowledge, negatively it can exhibit pessimism, foolhardiness and unnecessary risk taking. Three is seen as a very magical number. In some cases, the number three can take on some negative aspects and is seen as demonic or unnatural, as there are no creatures in our world who walk upon three legs.

12.4. FOUR

Four derives its significance from various sources. It is the first "composite" number; that is to say, the first number that can be created from multiplying numbers other than itself and 1, in that $2 \times 2 = 4$. The simplest solid object — a tetrahedron — has four sides; hence four denotes solid matter in general and the Earth in particular, as the Earth is a solid object bounded by four cardinal points (North, South, East and West).

Time is another concept strongly associated with four, on the grounds that the year has four seasons and the month has (roughly) four weeks; Christian-oriented observers also note that the life story of Jesus is told in four gospels, each of which is in turn linked to one of the four classical "elements" of fire, air, earth, and water.

The association with Earth means that four symbolises being practical and "down-to-earth," while the fact that four is the first composite number is linked to the idea of an other-directed, "composite personality" that takes cues from different and often conflicting sources, leading to fiercely independent, "out-of-the-box" thinking.

12.5. FIVE

Five is connected to sensual awareness in the form of the five senses as well as protection. It is also a number which represents service to others. It is highly analytical and has the ability to think critically, but can over-ponder an issue to the point that its significance is no longer relevant. This number governs our ability to think clearly and our intellectual capacity. Five represents openness to new experiences as well as new ideas. Seeking freedom, it is often the adventurer. Five is about pushing life to its limits. It is a multifaceted number with links to our state of physical and mental health.

12.6. SIX

Six relates to tact, beauty and harmony. It is very much a relationship builder which corresponds to one-to-one encounters. It deals with that which we are attracted to and those things we find great pleasure in. Six possesses charm, grace and the ability to make small talk on any stratum, and is therefore much of a diplomat. Six is very nurturing, and is considered the mother/father number. It is considered to be a minor money number, so a little extra income will be available wherever this number is found. Negatively, six can be unfaithful, jealous, bitter and vengeful. Six can also denote perfectionism. The name number of Bharat, Brahma and Shiv are 6.

12.7. SEVEN

Seven is considered to be a spiritual number because it is illusive and contains veils which must first be uncovered, one after another, before illumination will ultimately be found. Seven is said to be sacred, and this is evidenced by the fact that there are seven days in the week, ancient texts such as Genesis propose that the earth was formed in seven phases, the ancient solar system consisted of seven luminaries, and some versions of the Kabbalah have seven sephiroth. While seven possesses qualities of dreaminess, spirituality and psychic awareness, negatively it can be dubious, deceptive and insincere.

12.8. EIGHT

Eight is considered to be the number of karmic influences

where we are called upon to pay debts incurred in this and previous lives. It represents hard work and lessons learned through experience, and can therefore be a difficult number for some because of the very restrictiveness of its nature. More than any other number, eight seeks money and material success. However, the hardships eight faces in pursuit of its rewards are extreme. Huge reversals in life are common for the eight. Because reputation and community standing are of paramount importance, those who have it figured prominently would be wise to lead honest lives, otherwise any indiscretions will more than likely be uncovered in a most unflattering manner. Although it is considered "good luck" in Chinese culture, it is of no particular importance according to the esoteric beliefs of Chinese numerology.

12.9. NINE

Nine was considered to be a sacred number by the ancients and was consequently not assigned a numerical equivalent to any letter in the Chaldean alphabet. It represents change, invention and growth which springs forth from inspiration. Nine is the humanitarian. Nine has traditionally held esoteric significance which is evidenced by the fact that it takes nine calendar months to bring a baby into the world from its initial conception.

The following chart will give the importance of this number.

Years of Satyug	1,728,000	9
Years of Treta Yug	1,296,000	9
Years of Dwapar Yug	864,000	9
Years of Kali Yug	432,000	9
Days of a Year	360	9
Number of Constellations	27	9
Number of Planets	9	9

12.10. TEN

Ten is a higher octave of the number one and signifies an end of an important cycle in which a change in circumstances will soon be forthcoming. It carries with it much esoteric significance which is evidenced by the fact that it takes ten lunar months to bring a baby from conception into the world, there are ten sephiroth in many versions of the Kaballah, the most common number system used today is based on the number ten, and most currencies in use today have been decimalised. This belief is also central to Chinese numerology. It should be noted that ten is considered to be the modern number of completion because it was only within the last several hundred years that is has been used as the fundamental building block of number systems, currencies and measurements. When ten replaced twelve as the ultimate number, it heralded a change in man's thinking patterns to become more scientific in his approach to questions of an esoteric nature.

10.11. ELEVEN

Eleven is a higher octave of the number two and is considered to be a master number (the second master number being 22). 11 is considered the path of spiritual awareness and knowledge beyond the grasp of others. It carries psychic vibrations and has an equal balance of masculine and feminine properties. It is also related to open-mindedness, intuition, idealism, and visions. Because eleven contains many gifts such as psychic awareness and a keen sense of sensitivity, it also has negative effects such as treachery and betrayal from secret enemies.

10.12. TWELVE

Twelve is a higher octave of the number three and is an

indicator of great understanding and wisdom. Much of its knowledge is gleaned from life experiences which enables a sense of calm to prevail in even the most turbulent of situations. Twelve is significant in ancient man's life because there were twelve tribes in Israel, twelve disciples followed Jesus, there are twelve astrological signs in the zodiac, there are twelve months in the year, and our modern clock is divided into two groups of twelve hours. It is considered to be the ancient number of completion as it signals the end of childhood and the beginning stages of adulthood.

Additionally, the ancient numbering and measuring systems are based on this number, as evidenced by terms such as a dozen (12), a gross (12 times 12), a shilling (12 pence) and a foot (12 inches). Negatively, twelve can suffer from a form of depression brought about by a feeling of resignation that life's events have transpired in such a way.

10.13. THIRTEEN

Thirteen is a higher octave of the number four and is one more than twelve, the ancient number of completion. Thirteen is considered to signify the end of a cycle, as evidenced by the fact that there are thirteen lunar months in the year and thirteen signs in the Celtic and Native American systems of astrology. While thirteen foretells new beginnings, it also signifies that outmoded systems must come to an end to make way for much needed transformations. Thirteen may also be interpreted as 12 + 1 and is regarded by many as the number of the initiate, this is seen in a chromatic musical octave. But thirteen's real significance cannot really be discussed without reference to sacred geometry, more particularly the Flower of Life, which is from the Temple of Osiris and shows the never ending destruction and creation of life. It is also very significant to the creation pattern and the platonic solids. Thirteen is also a significant astrological number. The sum of thirteen is 96, (1+2+3..), which is each number of days in a season.

10.14. TWENTY-TWO

Twenty-two is a higher octave of the number four and is considered to be a master number. It contains the secrets to many esoteric questions, as evidenced by the fact that there are twenty two letters in the Hebrew alphabet, twenty two pathways in many versions of the Kaballah, and twenty two cards in the Major Arcana. Twenty two carries with it psychic gifts such as heightened sensitivity, intuition and psychic awareness, but is also predisposed to pitfalls such as treachery from hidden enemies and over sensitivity. It is also an approximation of pi times 7, and also the number of pounds in 10 kilograms.

10.15. ZERO

Zero is a powerful number which brings great transformational change, sometimes occurring in a profound manner. It has much intensity, so caution is needed wherever it appears to ensure that extremes are not encountered.

10.16. ALPHABETIC HARMONICS

In contrast to the verbal society we currently live in, mythical ancient civilisations such as Atlantis and Lemuria are believed by some to have had a slightly different means of communication which was composed on an elaborate system, including art forms which conveyed special messages to the observer. In our current age of known history, early man recorded events which transpired by using pictorial representations which told elaborate stories. As time went on these pictures were abbreviated to form hieroglyphics with each symbol depicting a word. As more time elapsed the glyphs were further reduced to represent individual sounds.

The alphabet that we use today is most likely derived from an earlier Egyptian hieroglyphic system which in turn was derived from a pictographic system, similar to the concept on which the Chinese and Japanese writing systems are based. As the hieroglyphics evolved to represent sounds instead of specific words, these letters as we now know them took on a complete essence of their own: so much so that the spelling of many words has remained unchanged even though our speech patterns have evolved to make some sounds obsolete.

As mankind's system of thought and style of communication evolved to become more verbalised, the concept began to become apparent that each sound conveys a particular harmonic vibration which has particular significance to the exoteric as well as esoteric implications of our milieu. Numerologists believe that every letter in the alphabet has a specific essence that can best be described by associating it with a numerical value, thereby allowing for ease of computation. Each letter in any given word helps to add a particular flavour in order to clarify its meaning: this is especially so when it is the first letter or multiple occurrences of a particular letter are found in a word. The premier, or first, consonant or vowel of a word tends to carry significant importance and these letters will often reveal the overall essence of a word or name.

A is the numerical equivalent of 1 and the first letter of the alphabet as well as the first vowel. It has a great deal of confidence which enables it to achieve objectives. When it is the first vowel in a name, the bearer tends to be alert and bold. Negatively, A can be critical of efforts of others.

B is the numerical equivalent of 2 and represents our emotional reactions. It is friendly, sympathetic and enjoys domesticity. Negatively, B can be self absorbed if not a bit greedy.

C is the numerical equivalent of 3 and represents energy. It is particularly good humoured and gets along well with others. Negatively, C can be unscrupulous and inattentive to the needs of others.

D is the numerical equivalent of 4 and represents balance. It is very powerful and is the letter associated with business. When it is the first consonant in a name the bearer will display a need for order and tidiness. Negatively, D can be stubborn and uncompromising.

E is the second vowel in the alphabet and is the numerical equivalent of 5. It is a friendly number which is warm hearted, loving and compassionate. When it is the first vowel in a name the bearer is freedom loving and charming. Negatively, E can be unreliable and unstable.

F is the numerical equivalent of 6 and represents love. It is warm-hearted, compassionate, and has the ability to make others feel at ease. When it is the first consonant in a name it carries the vibration of a mother hen type of individual. Negatively, F can carry a sense of melancholy.

G is the numerical equivalent of 7 and represents mysticism and religious experiences. This letter is imaginative, creative, and will look for alternative solutions to everyday problems. When it is the first consonant in a name, the bearer will tend to be intuitive, learned and somewhat solitary. Negatively, G's are loathe to take even the best intentioned advice from others.

H is the numerical equivalent of 8 and represents creativity and power. This letter has a great deal of business acumen and will therefore find profits through most endeavours. When it is the first consonant of a name the bearer is likely to be successful in business. Negatively, it can be self absorbed and selfish.

I is the third vowel of the alphabet and is the numerical equivalent of 9. It represents law and as a general rule is sensitive, compassionate and humane. Negatively, I can lack self confidence and is quick to anger.

J is the numerical equivalent of 1 and represents our aspirations. This letter is truthful, benevolent and intelligent. When it is the first consonant in a name the bearer will possess an unyielding desire not to give up and will therefore find success - eventually. Negatively, J can be lazy and lack direction.

K is the numerical equivalent of 2 and represents extremes. It is strong willed and influential, if not somewhat emotive at times. When it is the first consonant of a name the bearer will possess insights often missed by others. Negatively, K can be dissatisfied with life.

L is the numerical equivalent of 3 and represents action. It is charitable and well adjusted but can be somewhat accident prone.

M is the numerical equivalent of 4 and represents spirituality. This letter has a great deal of self confidence and is therefore likely to achieve success. It is also an industrious letter that can be somewhat of a workaholic. Negatively, M can be hasty and quick to anger.

N is the numerical equivalent of 5 and represents imagination. It is intuitive and communicative, but negatively can be predisposed to jealousy.

O is the penultimate vowel and equates to the number 6. This letter represents patience and is particularly studious. When it is the first vowel in a name, the person will be community minded and a good student. Negatively, O needs to learn to gain greater control over its emotions.

P is the numerical equivalent of 7 and represents power. It carries with it a commanding influence and possesses much knowledge. When it is the first consonant in a name the bearer is likely to think of spiritual matters. Negatively, P can be totally self absorbed with little time to empathise with the concerns of others.

Q is the numerical equivalent of 8 and represents originality. It is a mysterious letter which in many ways shows areas that would otherwise be unknowable. Negatively, Q can be extremely boring.

R is the numerical equivalent of 9 and represents possibilities. It is tolerant and humane but has a tendency to become short tempered. When it is the first consonant in a name the bearer will often act as peacemaker.

S is the numerical equivalent of 1 and represents beginnings. It has very attractive attributes and instils wealth. Negatively, S can act impulsively and cause massive upheavals to occur.

T is the numerical equivalent of 2 and represents growth. It is a restless letter which seeks answers to spiritual questions. When it is the first consonant in a name, the carrier will have extra strength to help other and tends to be long suffering. Negatively, T is overly emotional and is often easily influenced by the opinions of others.

U is the final true vowel in the alphabet and is the numerical equivalent of 3. This letter represents accumulation and is considered to be very lucky indeed. When it is the first vowel in a name the bearer will be freedom loving. Negatively, U can be selfish, greedy and indecisive.

V is the numerical equivalent of 4 and represents construction. It is an industrial letter which is tireless and efficient. Negatively, V can be unpredictable.

W is the numerical equivalent of 5 and represents self-expression. While this letter can be exceedingly charming, it also possesses an aura of mystique. Negatively, W can be greedy and take too many risks.

X is the antepenultimate letter in our alphabet and is the numerical equivalent of 6. It represents sexuality. This letter is unrestrained in its quest for pleasure and can therefore fall prey to promiscuity and unfaithfulness.

Y is the penultimate letter in our alphabet and is the numerical equivalent of 7. This letter represents freedom and dislikes restraint of any kind. Negatively, Y can be indecisive and as a consequence may miss out on opportunities in life.

Z is the final letter in our alphabet and is the numerical equivalent of 8. It represents hope as it is considered to be a peacemaker. Negatively, Z can be headstrong and must learn to think before acting.

10.17. NUMEROLOGICAL DIVINATION

The basis of the belief that dates and times have numerologic significance appears to be that underlying vibrations of the universe as a whole occur in regular cycles and that things created or changed at one or another point in these cycles will express the properties which the vibrations at that point in the cycle create. It is less clear how names, words and appellations would follow such a rule. One theory put forward by some numerologists is that persons who name things are subtly affected by universal vibrations to assign appropriate names which harmonise with the vibrations of the thing named.

Another question which has been asked relative to the numerological significance of words is how, if letters can be assigned numbers, things can have a uniform numerological identity when they are named differently in different languages and with different alphabets. For example, the numerologic value for "shirt" in English would be 8. The same item in Spanish would be "camisa," a 6 in numerology. One theory to explain this apparent inconsistency is that the different names for an object in different languages and orthographies correspond to different distinctive qualities of that object, just as different words for the same thing in the same language can carry different connotations.

To date, there is no scientific verification for the validity of claimed numerological principles. Numerology has thus been classified as a pseudoscience, and most scientists regard it as either deluded quackery or deliberate fraud. True science, as recognised in modern society, is based on the scientific method and requires that assertions answer to the regular and replicable use of this method to be considered as scientifically verifiable fact.

Numerologists reply that their study does not answer to science as the mechanisms of interaction between universal vibration and gross physical things are too subtle to be detected, measured or quantified by tools currently available to science. However, given that numerologists make predictions about observable events, scientists would argue that the simultaneous claim that science cannot detect any effects is illogical. Empirical observations relating to the regular and predictable mathematical relationships between things in the universe are pointed to as evidence of a numerological fabric underlying all things. However, such observations give no direct support to numerology's claims.

Numerology is by no means a unified study. Proponents of its veracity may be generally divided into three schools. With limited elaboration:

Numerology is true by Divine fiat and contains clues placed into the fabric of the universe by the Almighty for the enlightened to decipher, thereby bringing them closer to unity with a Grand Plan.

Numerology is true because of universal spiritual agreement between all life on one level or another. And because the Universe is the product of the mean (as in statistical mean) agreement between all of life everywhere, the agreement on mathematical regularity in the universe creates a Numerological sub-fabric throughout the universe.

Numerology is true because it is a reflection of Natural Law, giving clues to the state of a complex of vibrations which regulate function and existence in the universe. The failure of modern science to verify this fact is merely a reflection of insufficient advances in science. After all, science once believed all matter was composed of earth, air, fire and water in different combinations. If and when science is sufficiently advanced, it will be able to verify the truth of numerology.

Historians believe that modern numerology is an integration of the teachings from Ancient Babylonia, Pythagoras and his followers, (6 th. Century B.C. Greece) Astrological philosophy from Hellenistic Alexandria, early Christian mysticism, the occultism of the early Gnostics and the Hebrew system of the Qabala. The Indian Vedas, the Chinese "Circle of the Dead",and the Egyptian "Book of the Master of the Secret House", (Ritual of the Dead) are records giving strong evidence that Numerology dates back thousands of years.

Pythagoras and other philosophers of the time believed that because mathematical concepts were more "practical" (easier to regulate and classify) than physical ones, they had greater actuality. This is an idea in harmony with philosophical pragmatism and a choice for permanent concepts over changeable physicality. A claim of numerology is that its practitioners, through empirical observation and investigation, have concluded that through the study of numbers man can uncover hidden aspects of himself and the universe.

Other Books on

OCCULT SCIENCE

1. Teach Yourself Vaastu (New)
2. Reiki The Science of Healing
3. The Marvels of Palmistry
4. Healing Power of Gems
5. Awake Kundalini
6. Learn Meditation
7. Teach Yourself Numerology
8. Teach Yourself Astrology
9. Teach Yourself Graphology
10. Teach Yourself Effectively Feng Shui

Unit No. 220, Second Floor, 4735/22,
Prakash Deep Building, Ansari Road, Darya Ganj,
New Delhi - 110002.
E-mail: lotuspress1984@gmail.com, www.lotuspress.co.in